CRASH COMMUNICATION

CRASH COMMUNICATION

MANAGEMENT TECHNIQUES FROM THE COCKPIT TO MAXIMIZE PERFORMANCE

PETER BRANDL

New York

CRASH COMMUNICATION
MANAGEMENT TECHNIQUES FROM THE COCKPIT TO MAXIMIZE PERFORMANCE

Published in New York, New York, by Morgan James Publishing. Morgan James and The Entrepreneurial Publisher are trademarks of Morgan James, LLC.
www.MorganJamesPublishing.com

The Morgan James Speakers Group can bring authors to your live event. For more information or to book an event visit The Morgan James Speakers Group at
www.TheMorganJamesSpeakersGroup.com.

The Original Edition "Crash Kommunikation - Warum Piloten versagen und Manager Fehler machen" was published in German by GABAL Verlag, Offenbach am Main in 2010.

Shelfie

A **free** eBook edition is available with the purchase of this print book.

CLEARLY PRINT YOUR NAME ABOVE IN UPPER CASE

Instructions to claim your free eBook edition:
1. Download the Shelfie app for Android or iOS
2. Write your name in **UPPER CASE** above
3. Use the Shelfie app to submit a photo
4. Download your eBook to any device

ISBN 978-1-63047-804-9 paperback
ISBN 978-1-63047-806-3 eBook
ISBN 978-1-63047-805-6 hardcover
Library of Congress Control Number:
2015915623

Cover Design by:
Chris Treccani
www.3dogdesign.net

In an effort to support local communities and raise awareness and funds, Morgan James Publishing donates a percentage of all book sales for the life of each book to Habitat for Humanity Peninsula and Greater Williamsburg.

Get involved today, visit
www.MorganJamesBuilds.com

Habitat
for Humanity®
Peninsula and
Greater Williamsburg
Building Partner

CONTENTS

PREFACE

The late 1970s saw a devastating accident involving two jumbo jets on Tenerife. Two airplanes full of passengers rammed into each other on the runway. The result: 583 killed—the worst civil aviation catastrophe of all time. How was it possible for two fully functioning planes to become the cause of such a devastating accident? Which factors had to come together in order to result in such a disaster?[1]

WHAT CREW RESOURCE MANAGEMENT MEANS

The new discipline "CRM" arose as a consequence of this accident. In aviation, CRM does not refer to Customer Relationship Management, but Crew Resource Management. Here, the focus is the question of why planes crash, even when they are in perfect working order and no technical malfunctions are present. In this context, there is frequent reference to "human failure," yet technically this designation is incorrect. It should actually be called "human precision." If I was standing next to you, and pinched your arm, you would very likely burst out: "Are you crazy?!" or "What the hell??" If I punched you in the stomach, you would double over; of that, I am 100 percent sure. Just like there are stimuli on the bodily level that inevitably lead to certain reactions, there are also stimuli on the psychological and behavioral

1   Xavier Waterkeyn, *Air Disasters of the World* (Munich: New Holland, 2007).

levels. When certain factors appear in a certain sequence, the corresponding reaction follows with the utmost probability and predictability. For that reason, the key question is this: what are the factors that lead to catastrophic consequences?

HOW AVIATION, MANAGEMENT, AND BUSINESS ARE RELATED

This is the question pursued by Crew Resource Management. In the wake of Tenerife, many answers that make flying safer have been found. Fascinatingly, many of these questions and answers convert nearly one to one to management or business life. This book is about the lessons managers and leaders can learn from the findings of catastrophe avoidance in aviation (and consequently, we can learn from fatal plane crashes too).

ABOUT THE AUTHOR

The idea of bringing together management and flying literally forces itself on someone at home in both worlds. As an executive and manager, I have frequently experienced how small breakdowns in communication can blow up into large problems. As an airline pilot, I analyzed numerous plane crashes during my training and have gone through Crew Resource Management myself. And as a trainer and management coach, I am reminded on a near-daily basis that companies rarely get into trouble due to dramatic external events. Here, too, mistakes in the company cockpit are almost always responsible for the crash. In that respect, crash prevention in business is just as possible as in aviation. But don't take my word for it!

—**Peter Brandl'**
Berlin, Germany, September 2015

INTRODUCTION
OF CRASHES AND THEIR CAUSES

HUMAN ERROR AND "HUMAN FACTORS"

More than three-quarters of all air accidents can be traced back to "human error" (i.e., not due to bad weather, material deficiency, or mistakes by ATC [Air Traffic Control]). "Human error"—we are all familiar with this formula from the evening news. It is frequently used when reporting on other accidents with many deaths, from severe traffic collisions to abnormal incidents in nuclear power stations. And there is almost always a note of recrimination to it; someone bears responsibility for the event because he acted improperly. The Anglo-American usage is more clear-sighted than the German. Rather than "failure," reference is made to "human factors" that lead to breakdowns and accidents. Put another way, "That's the way humans are." Humans overlook or misinterpret things; they make hasty decisions—especially under stress. They are paralyzed by fear or ignore obvious dangers. To put it bluntly, shit happens.

Let us return once more to the devastating crash on Tenerife. It gave the aviation industry the impetus to systematically analyze human factors, influences, and limitations. How can it be that two experienced pilots, both in full possession of their mental faculties, let two technically fully functional airplanes crash into each other on the ground? The barely believable becomes understandable when we consider the following factors.

Tenerife: Unfortunate Factors

- Both aircraft, a KLM jet from Amsterdam and a Pan Am jet from New York, had been forced to land on Tenerife. Their actual destination airport on Gran Canaria had been shut down at short notice due to a bomb threat.
- Both aircraft were Boeing 747s, a large plane that could only taxi on the runway at Tenerife Los Rodeos, because it was too wide for the taxiway (parallel to the runway).
- Fog gathered as the planes waited at the overcrowded airport.
- Air traffic control directed both aircraft to the only runway. Both crews (and air traffic control) knew of each other. They knew that they were in the immediate vicinity of the other aircraft, but had no visual contact. There was no ground radar.
- The Pan Am crew was unfamiliar with the airport. This, and the malfunction of the center light strip on the runway, led them to miss the decisive turn-off to leave the runway and line up behind the KLM when air traffic control attempted to guide them off it.
- The captain of the KLM (who was, incidentally, KLM's most senior pilot and head instructor for Boeing 747) misunderstood an order from air traffic control, possibly due to the controller's strong Spanish accent. Although air traffic control gave "route clearance," they had not given "takeoff clearance" because the position of the Pan Am plane was unclear. Only after the Tenerife airport disaster were distinct phrases for both instructions introduced.[2]
- The KLM captain was already three-and-a-half hours behind schedule. This meant he was running the risk of exceeding the maximum permitted on-duty time. If he did, he would have to spend the night on Tenerife

---

2   Today a *Route Clearance* sounds like this: "KLM 999, you are cleared to Frankfurt via X and Y"; a *Takeoff Clearance* sounds like this: "KLM 999, you are cleared for takeoff, runway 09."

and, with him, all of his passengers. So the captain was under pressure and wanted to take off.

- The KLM co-pilot did not raise any objections, possibly because he simply did not trust himself to contradict such an experienced pilot. This was the training captain, after all, and something of an aviation demigod in Holland.

WAS THE COLLISION AVOIDABLE?

All this ultimately led the KLM plane to start the takeoff roll. It was already too late when both pilots saw each other at a distance of circa 700 meters. Although the Pan Am plane still tried to leave the runway and the KLM captain attempted to wrench his aircraft from the ground, the result was a crash causing almost 600 deaths.

When cases like these are being investigated, one can often read press reports about a "series of unfortunate events": the closure of another airport, the bad weather, the identical size of the aircraft, the conditions on Tenerife (only one suitable runway), and the time pressure. Yet, questions still remain: What would have happened if . . . ?

What Would Have Happened—Counter Questions

- What would have happened if the co-pilot of the KLM aircraft had contradicted the captain?
- What would have happened if the cockpit crew of the Pan Am plane had raised the alarm with air traffic control? ("We don't know where we are!")
- What would have happened if the Spanish flight controller had spoken better English?
- What would have happened if the KLM captain had asked the Spanish air traffic control to repeat the decisive order, just to be sure?
- What would have happened if the KLM captain had inquired, to be on the safe side, if the runway was clear: "It's a good plan if I can only see 700 meters but need 3 kilometers to take off, right?"
- What would have happened if the pilot of the KLM plane had stated, audible for everyone, "KLM, beginning takeoff!"?

THE ROLE OF COMMUNICATION

If only one of these possibilities had been put into action, then the story would have had a different ending. In the worst case, the KLM crew and their passengers would have had to stay the night, and this might have upset some passengers. However, the crash probably would have been prevented, and everyone would have survived. So the actual cause of the devastating crash was not the fog or defective runway lighting. The true cause was a breakdown in communication.

BREAKDOWNS IN COMPANIES

What does this all have to do with you and the work piled on your desk? Perhaps you can recall the last severe breakdown that happened at work. It's possible the causes were similarly banal and "human." It is possible that you too wanted to meet a target "come hell or high water," thereby systematically ignoring warning signals and doubts. Even high-profile executives are not above this. Think, for instance, of Juergen Schrempp, who was still tinkering with his "world corporation" long after it became clear to outsiders, as well as company members, that the DaimlerChrysler-Mitsubishi alliance was not working. Or take Wendelin Wiedeking, CEO of Porsche, who refused to budge an inch from his daring plan of a Volkswagen takeover, weighing down Porsche with billions in debt and ultimately serving his company up to VW on a plate. Or think of the local small businessman who opens up a cheese or wine shop a stone's throw from the established competition, almost guaranteeing failure. In retrospect, all three seem to have had their vision clouded, similar to the pilots on Tenerife.

CONSEQUENCES OF HUMAN MISTAKES

The mistakes caused by human factors have differing consequences. What "only" costs money and jobs in the case of a fishmonger, or in automobile production, can be life-threatening in other areas. That is why the attempt is made in safety-critical fields, such as aviation, the chemicals industry, hospitals, or nuclear power plants, to better control human factors through training. Astonishingly, human factors have yet to play a role in "normal" commercial enterprises. However, tunnel vision, mistakes, inability to act, or doing things for the sake of doing things can also have "life-threatening" consequences for a company—and, quite simply, lead to bankruptcy.

WHAT LEADS TO INSOLVENCY?

Anyone seeking the causes of a bankruptcy often encounters explanations such as "low equity ratio" or a "lack of liquidity." That is approximately the same as saying that planes crash because mountains get in the way or the fuel runs out. It is clearly easier to pick out the final symptoms than to dig deeper for the true causes. How is it that some managers work their way towards bankruptcy without a care in the world? Even insolvency administrators, a rather sober occupational group, introduce "soft" factors when probing for the causes of bankruptcy. A study from the year 2006 interviewed 125 insolvency administrators and came to the following conclusions:

- 96 percent of insolvency administrators believe that businessmen nourished the hope that things would somehow get better on their own.
- 95 percent consider fear of being exposed to ridicule among acquaintances or in the industry to be a reason why insolvency is delayed.
- 88 percent thought the situation was categorized as a mere crisis—not an insolvency—for too long.[3]

HUMAN NATURE: NEARLY UNCHANGED

"What happens is irrational," commented Professor Georg Bitter from the Centre for Insolvency and Recapitalization at the University of Mannheim (ZIS), which was commissioned by the credit insurance company Euler Hermes to conduct the survey. Conclusions like these always carry a note of surprise: how can it be that humans in the twenty-first century react so irrationally? Yet surprise is misplaced as our basic biological equipment has changed little in the past few millennia. Our perceptions or reflexes or biological possibilities are still the same as those of our ancestors. Evolution moves in very long cycles—even if some seem to believe that babies now are born complete with super-dexterous "mobile-phone thumbs."

OUR WORLD: DRASTICALLY CHANGED

In contrast, our environment has changed radically. One only has to look back 100 to 150 years—a blink of an eye from the evolutionary perspective. While our great-great-great grandparents still had to wait weeks for the mail coach for a letter to be

---

3   *Wirtschaft Konkret*, no. 414, www.wirtschaft-konkret.de/de/insolvenzursachen.html.

delivered, today, emails fly back and forth by the second. While our grandmothers still stoked the kitchen stove, you now need to study computer science if you want to master contemporary high-tech kitchens. And while our ancestors went to bed with the chickens due to a lack of electricity and in light of hard physical labor, today we can choose from numerous entertainment options, night after night. If letters used to be typed in good time at the office, almost every manager today is confronted by an overflowing email inbox, a telephone that rings incessantly, one meeting that chases the next, at least three employees who have "important" questions, and the fact that the agenda for the board meeting should have been prepared long ago.

In the "company cockpits," it is hardly less stressful than in the cockpit of a modern airplane. And a cockpit does not just appear to display more information than a normal human can handle; it is a fact. As a pilot, I know what I'm talking about. In the summer of 2006 the German magazine *Der Spiegel* curtly stated that "technical progress overwhelms the human capacity for orientation" in its title story, "Living with Fear."[4] Every day, you are confronted with more and more information, and the processes created by modern technology are getting faster and faster, and you have to deal with it somehow. There is little chance that this process will be reversed.

LEARNING FROM AVIATION

To be fair, the aviation industry devotes a considerable amount of effort to developing strategies that enable us to master this complexity, despite our obsolete biological hardware. How can we reduce complexity, summarize information, and avoid disastrous mistakes—even if humans are still just as influenced by emotions as our ancestors and our perception just as limited? You would search for these kinds of strategies in the business world in vain, excepting high-risk industries such as nuclear and chemicals. We humans are missing the "operating instructions for life in the twenty-first century," and many managers are missing a strategic safety net that protects them from "human error" during the working day. This book will give you the help you need to develop these safety mechanisms for your daily business life.

---

4   *Der Spiegel,* no. 35 (2006): 153.

CHAPTER 1

FORGETTING TO EXTEND THE FLAPS

(Or What Happens during Extreme Stress)

+ + + August 20, 2008, Madrid-Barajas Airport + + + A Spanair aircraft crashes immediately after takeoff and bursts into flames. + + + 154 casualties + + +

Eyewitnesses speak of "hell" and an "inferno." The MD-82, belonging to the Spanish airline Spanair, crashed in a riverbed only a few kilometers from Madrid's international airport shortly after takeoff. Of the 172 people on board, 154 died in the flames. There was initial speculation about engine failure, but a few weeks later, the actual cause of the crash was determined: the cockpit crew had forgotten to extend the flaps at takeoff. As a result, the aircraft failed to gain sufficient elevation.

Experts point to a "technical defect" because the alarm system designed for this scenario failed. But the extension of the flaps during takeoff and landing is actually a completely routine affair, which every pilot can perform in his sleep. For pilots, "extending flaps" before takeoff is as much a matter of routine as putting on your shoes before you leave the house. How is it possible to "forget" something like this?

MAIN SOURCE OF MISTAKES: STRESS

All of us have made mistakes that were so idiotic, so dumb that we breathed a sigh of relief that no one had been watching. "Human error" is not limited to pilots; when the critical factors come together, we are all capable of terrible mistakes. With a little luck, it remains just a close shave, like when we run a red light while preoccupied or leave our bank card in the cash machine. In the aviation industry, these kinds of mistakes can have devastating consequences—and in the business world too. One of the most significant factors that leads to the worst mistakes is simply stress.

CRASH EXAMPLE: MADRID, 2008

Function of Flaps

To understand the Spanair accident, you have to know how an airplane works. You will probably have seen how an airplane extends its flaps while taking off or landing. These flaps increase the surface area of the wing, increasing the lift that makes the airplane fly. Lift is ultimately derived from two factors, namely the surface of the wing and the speed of the air flowing around the wing. At takeoff and landing, the airplane is naturally slower, making the use of flaps necessary. Without flaps, the plane does not fly. Every pilot knows that; therefore, "extending the flaps" is utterly routine.

Reasons for Aborted Takeoffs

What exactly happened then? The crew had already been through two aborted takeoffs. Consider this picture of an aborted takeoff: The airplane is on the runway.

The engines are starting up, and the plane accelerates at full throttle. Meanwhile, various parameters are checked within the cockpit. Certain values have to be displayed. Various indicator lights light up as well. Each of these little lights indicates that the system represented is working. If one of these values is incorrect or an indicator does not light up in time, then the takeoff has to be aborted. In almost all cases, the pilots could have proceeded with the flight in perfect safety; a bulb had gone, nothing more. So an aborted takeoff is normally only a precautionary measure. However, the passengers don't know that. They just notice that the plane accelerates strongly and then the brakes are slammed on, almost lifting them out of their seats.

Further Obstacles

Due to false alarms, our crew already had two of these aborted takeoffs behind them. You can picture for yourself how the passengers would be starting to get restless. A situation like this is exacerbated by other factors like "slots," or a crew's rest period. A slot is a window of time in which the plane has to take off, for instance. If this doesn't work, then the crew has to apply for a new slot. If you have bad luck, then you might have to wait for several hours. But the mandatory rest periods can make this process tricky. The maximum duty time of a crew is strictly limited. If, for instance, a flight cannot be completed within the maximum on-duty time, due to delays or a missed slot, a new crew has to be found. You can imagine the problems this might cause when a plane is stuck at a random airport anywhere in the world.

A Risky Situation

That's how the explosive cocktail in Madrid was mixed: two aborted takeoffs; 162 restless and rebellious passengers (the next takeoff had to work out); extreme time pressure; extreme pressure to succeed; a whole series of external factors that ramped up the pressure to immeasurable levels. It was a recipe for stress and distress. All this led to an awful, careless mistake, and the pilot simply did not extend the flaps. If the warning system had worked properly, an alarm would have sounded and made the crew aware of their mistake, and 150 people would have departed safely. But it did not. Worse, recklessly, the crew had failed to work through the takeoff checklist; they had neglected their SOPs, their standard operating procedures.

CRASH WARNING

Above a certain level of stress, our behavior is no longer under rational control. It becomes reactive and unconsidered, rather than reflective; our actions become increasingly quick and agitated.

COMPANY EXAMPLE: KFW—A BANK GIVES AWAY €320 MILLION

To repeat: every one of us will have made some massive mistakes at some point in our lives. But what has to happen in order for a *company* to lose its "head"? What has to happen for a German state-owned bank like KfW to transfer €320 million to a bankrupt company, the funds never to be seen again? And what has to happen for a small or medium enterprise to lose control of its decision-making process and start making hasty and ill-considered decisions?

KfW: Busts, Breakdowns, and Bad Luck

The story of KfW bank is well known in Germany. In September 2008, it unleashed a storm of outrage. Although the crisis at the American investment bank Lehman Brothers was common knowledge, even to those who skip past the business section, KfW still transferred over €300 million to the insolvent company on September 15, 2008. No one had stopped the automated transfer in time. For a long time, it seemed extremely unlikely that German taxpayers would ever see any of their money again. It was announced in December 2009 that KfW was to get €200 million back (the German taxpayers had to find the remaining €120 million). Some context: at this point, KfW had already been coming under fire for months, primarily due to a debacle at the highly indebted IKB bank (KfW held 43 percent of the stock). KfW had to repeatedly bail out IKB and reported losses of €6.2 billion for the 2007 financial year, the largest loss in company history. Board member Ingrid Matthäus-Maier was forced first to quit as spokeswoman, then resign from the company altogether. The new chairman, Ulrich Schröder, had only been in the position for two weeks at the time of the incident. You can picture how, in these circumstances, the venerable KfW bank bore a closer resemblance to a henhouse with a fox on the loose than a well-organized institution. Enormous public pressure, a new chairman, and almost certainly worry about jobs and standing on the corporate ladder raised stress levels for every employee. Under these circumstances, it is actually not surprising that, despite a meeting on Friday, no one took decisive steps to prevent Monday's "accident."

Stress-Related Mistakes Everywhere

Such mishaps are not restricted to giant corporations or particular branches of industry. One well-known publishing house forgot to book its stand for the Frankfurt Book Fair, the most crucial industry event in Europe. The Social Democratic Party (SPD, one of the major parties in Germany) forgot to nominate its sitting mayor for election in Wiesbaden. It only came to light when the candidate and city deacon had already resigned from his position at the church and the campaign was underway. I was not a fly on the wall at the decisive KfW meeting that Friday, nor was I party to the internal workings of the SPD electoral machine in Wiesbaden. But wouldn't you say, too, that both debacles are fatally reminiscent of the flaps forgotten by the Spanair pilots? In all three cases, those involved were under a high level of stress.

STRESS AND ITS CONSEQUENCES

Humans: Beings Blessed by Reason

Why can stress be so devastating? Why do people who are normally rational and competent make such glaring mistakes, forgetting the obvious? Why do we overlook things that we would never overlook under normal circumstances? Questions like this emerge because "human error" contradicts the self-image we like to cultivate in everyday life. After all, we normally regard ourselves as rational beings who react "reasonably" to our surroundings, analyze them logically, and assess them reliably. *Homo sapiens* are ultimately creatures blessed with reason. This premise is particularly true in the business context, in the world of managers, movers, and shakers. The idea has been anchored in the European history of ideas since the eighteenth century, in the understanding that humans are controlled by their "ratio." "I think, therefore I am," Descartes said. Kant challenged individuals to follow the path of enlightenment and gave them the (for him) unusually simple advice: "Have the courage to make use of your own reason."

Humans: The Emotional Being

This optimistic conception of humanity has been increasingly shaken and called into question by modern science. Neurology and brain research suggest that humans are emotionally driven and directed by subconscious influences. It is becoming increasingly clear how selective our perception is and how prejudiced we are in our judgments and assessments. The irrationality people are capable of is made painfully obvious by the shocking mistakes we can make under stress.

A Typical Stress Reaction: Say Goodbye to your Cerebrum

Maybe you can remember the last time you were under great stress yourself. I do not mean the usual time pressure under which most of us constantly find ourselves in our everyday lives, the type that leaves us complaining about "stress" when winding down with a drink in the evening. Rather, I mean a situation you perceived as actually threatening, perhaps even experienced as terrifying: a severe conflict in an important board meeting; a downed server that stops the entire company in its tracks; the news that your biggest customer is insolvent. You probably became flushed, your pulse accelerated, and your heartbeat began thudding in your ears. You may have felt unable to think clearly. Did you feel frozen? Maybe you had a blackout. It seems as if it is hardest to keep a cool head when we need to most.

Brainstem versus Cerebrum

The brainstem takes control in acute stress situations. This is the area of our brain in which the vital functions and basic emotions are located. The brainstem is sometimes also known as the "reptile brain." From an evolutionary standpoint, this is the most ancient part of the brain, where archaic patterns of behavior are stored; it is designed to ensure survival at all costs. The possibilities are few: fight, flight, or play dead. Those are the three exact options that were available to prehistoric humans when they encountered a saber-toothed tiger. The cerebrum, which is responsible for thought, analysis, and planning, is in large part shut down by acute stress. In my seminars, I am fond of saying, "When the brainstem comes, the cerebrum goes to the bar for a drink." And as soon as the cerebrum takes a break, people can overlook things that they would never neglect otherwise—for instance, extending the landing flaps or double-checking a multi-million-euro bank transfer.

When the Focus Shifts

Rüdiger Trimpop, professor of work, business, and organization psychology at Friedrich Schiller University, Jena, is one of the most renowned accident researchers in Germany. He offers the following impressive examples: "It is well-known from research on stress and accidents that humans develop tunnel vision in decision-making situations under time pressure." Trimpop recalls air traffic controllers who, in a simulated, stressful work situation (monitor failure, boss yelling, static noise from the speakers), were able to direct the airplane they were responsible for safely to the ground, but completely overlooked a collision of two other aircraft on their screen. "All their energy, their entire attention, is concentrated on that one task, and everything else is ignored. And the more complex an activity is, the greater the likelihood of focusing on the wrong thing." That is true not only for air traffic controllers under pressure, but also for motorists, who will overlook cyclists coming towards them on a one-way street. The accident researcher's advice: "It's a question of making sure to stop yourself from reacting as a reflex amoeba."[5]

Controlled Stress

As long as we still believe we can come to grips with a challenging situation, then a stress reaction can be controlled. Environmental stimuli put the brain on alert: the adrenal glands pour adrenaline into the blood; the heart begins to beat more quickly; we tense up and mobilize all of our energy. You might have felt that way during the last test you had to pass. As soon as you solved the first task, answered the first problem, you started to calm down.

Uncontrolled Stress

The contrasting reaction in our bodies when we struggle with an uncontrollable stress response is vividly described by the renowned neurobiologist Gerald Hüther: "When all the pathways are blocked or obstructed, the sirens sound in addition to the alarms . . . cold sweat drips from our brow. All hell is let loose in our brain, there's a total state of confusion." The pituitary gland then releases a hormone, which causes the adrenal glands to release large amounts of the stress hormone cortisol. "The initial fear turns into despair, powerlessness, helplessness. The stress

---

5   Peter Laudenbach, "Augenblicke der Freiheit" (Moments of Freedom), *Brand eins*, no. 3 (2008): 116; here 120–121.

reactions taking place in the body can no longer be stopped . . . We keep searching in vain for a solution, or wait for a miracle to happen and everything to go back to how it was." Subsequently, resignation, despondency, and "a feeling of unrest and paralysis" spread.[6] This is a state in which we can neither pass a test nor fly a plane nor safely lead a company.

Stress in Companies

Stress Is Relative

What is considered to be stressful varies from one person to the next—not all situations are as clear-cut as the saber-toothed tiger. What does not vary is the feeling of a loss of control, of being overwhelmed. Stimuli that appear without warning, like possible threats or the unknown, cause stress. When someone suddenly jumps in front of you as you are walking home through a dark alley late at night; if your conversation partner, friendly just a moment before, suddenly rolls up his sleeves and starts giving you the "death stare"; or when you—as a decidedly non-athletic person—are suddenly expected to acrobatically traverse a forest rope course at great heights in a management seminar, you will very likely feel stressed. However, a colleague who is a passionate free climber will look forward to it, and the boxer Vladimir Klitschko would probably perceive the situation in the dark alley differently than the actress Vivien Leigh.

Practice How to Control Stress

Therefore, it is not the situation itself that is "stressful" but rather the evaluation of the situation by the individual. In many cases, people will agree in their evaluation (saber-toothed tigers and other serious threats, for instance), but in others, the perception of the situation depends on previous experience and training. For instance, think about your first driving lessons. For many people, those were 60 extremely stressful minutes, after which they stepped out of the car, completely exhausted and with a stiff neck. Today, you look back and laugh. The situation, unfamiliar at the time, has long since become routine. Therefore, practice and training can help you experience a stressful situation as manageable and, thus, help

---

6   Gerald Hüther, *Biologie der Angst. Wie aus Stress Gefühle werden* (The Biology of Fear: How Emotions Arise from Stress) (Göttingen: Vandenhoeck and Ruprecht, 2007), 36.

you handle it well. It is not without reason that pilots repeatedly practice dangerous situations in a flight simulator. This can give us hope; it is possible to train for all dicey moments that are imaginable or predictable. And with a little luck, this training prevents the cerebellum from taking a nap if the worst comes to worst.

Types of Stressors

Maybe you're asking yourself by now what saber-toothed tigers, rope courses, or muggers in dark alleys have to do with your daily life as a manager. Of course, the danger of encountering a carnivore in the office hallway is relatively low. The stressors in a business are of a different nature, but no less potent. Today there is a consensus in stress research that in addition to "objective stressors" (like heat, cold, noise, sleep deprivation, injury, or acute danger), there are also "subjective stressors" that have a strong effect. Such subjective stressors include, for example, worries arising from a fundamentally negative attitude or a strongly perceived pressure to perform as a result of perfectionism. The same is true for "social stressors." Rüdiger Trimpop warns that "emotional conflicts, overload, and excessive complexity can cause consequences similar to stress and time pressure." The mathematician and financial psychologist Franz Reither, who wrote a very readable book about "complexity management," takes the same line: "Loss of control and hence stress aren't just a result of things 'getting out of hand.' Plain uncertainty and lack of predictability are enough to put things out of balance."[7]

Causes of Stress

Therefore, stress at work also arises under these circumstances:

- When people don't know how to proceed
- When people can't evaluate what is going on around them
- When one's own self-worth is threatened by new developments (for example, through conflicts with superiors, colleagues, or employees)
- When people have the feeling that they can no longer control a situation

---

7   Franz Reither, *Komplexitätsmanagement. Denken und Handeln in Komplexen Situationen* (Management of Complexity: Thinking and Acting in Complex Situations) (Munich: Gerling Academy Publishing, 1997), 110.

Stressful Situations at Work

So now we are closing in on typical business situations and their effects on employees. Companies are restructured, changing not just areas of responsibility, but teams as well. A merger with a competitor is planned, and no one can guess what the effect will be on his own job. Decreasing sales figures intensify competition, internally as well as externally. Often, it is simply the increased complexity of tasks in a globalized high-tech economy that causes the feelings of powerlessness and overload, and thus stress. If you are aware of these processes, then conduct within companies can be explained through the paradigm of brainstem-driven reflexes.

Flight as a Reaction to Stress

For instance, take the manager of a medium-sized machine tools manufacturer that is in a deep crisis. Sales have taken a tumble, cheap competition from the Far East is stealing market share, and to top it all off, an important customer canceled his contract. Insolvency no longer seems out of the question. One would think that the manager in this precarious situation would be working day and night to restructure the business. Yet, instead, he gives into a request for a time-intensive honorary post and is barely around. He eagerly dives into the public side and is actively involved in the organization's public relations—from the selection of images to the meticulous correction of punctuation in the latest flyer(!). He's not too important for any task. Running away is a classic flight reaction—and as might be expected, one that meets with little success. The company has to file for insolvency and is taken over by a competitor.

Playing Dead as a Reaction to Stress

Or take, for instance, the numerous companies with pedigrees reaching back decades, which, at some point, fall behind the times and steer towards disaster with eyes wide open. This is how Märklin focused undaunted on model railways long after PlayStations and computers had entered kids' rooms, and, practically speaking, their only customer base was middle-aged men. The company had to register insolvency. The watchmaker Junghans also failed to make the transition, although the company was being put under increasing pressure by cheap competition. "The company was too late in switching from mass production to high-quality watches," the *Frankfurter Rundschau* judged. The company was sold to an investor in January

2009.[8] It was not an unanticipated crisis that finished off the traditional brand, but rather a slow process, to which the owners clearly closed their eyes. In both companies, the sales department will have reported sinking sales figures from year to year. The accounting departments will have registered shrinking profits and, at some point, losses. But the management apparently practiced an "ostrich policy." One might put it this way: they played dead.

Fight as a Reaction to Stress

Reflexively going on the offensive is nothing new for managers. One example: A mid-size media company goes public. Although the initial public offering brings the expected capital into the coffers, the boldly initiated projects—including the entry into film and consultancy business—consume huge sums and produce only meager sales. As the stock price goes down further and further, on top of it all, the chairman and cofounder of the company instigates a lawsuit against one of the principal shareholders. From his perspective, the shareholder was interfering with his management of the business and arrogating far too much power. Subsequently, the press reports more about the latest developments in this legal dispute than the company's products. The consequence: negative headlines without end, decreasing sales, and the stock loses even more value. The lawsuit, which concerned the exclusion of a group of investors associated with the principal shareholder from the company's general meeting of shareholders, is lost. The company initially survives, but the new board has to let go of employees, cut programs, and reduce costs wherever possible. This can be called wild attacking—regardless of the cost.

ANTI-CRASH FORMULA

Ask yourself occasionally, especially in the difficult situations, "Who is in charge right now: cerebrum or brainstem?"

THE PITFALLS OF HUMAN PERCEPTION

Examples like these leave many observers speechless: can the people involved not see the damage they are doing? The sales figures are right there on the table. You

---

8   "Krise frisst Erinnerungen" (Crisis Eats Memories), *Frankfurter Rundschau*, no. 3 (February 11, 2009).

would think that the negative press reports would be as impossible to ignore as the piles of made-in-China clocks at the local supermarket or at the latest trade fair. This leads us to an awkward question: how real is real?

How Real Is Real?

"Objective" Perception of the World

How Real Is Real is the provocative title of a book by Paul Watzlawick. The well-known philosopher and theorist on the psychology of communication was a radical "constructivist." Watzlawick's answer to the title's question is simply this: the world is not *how* it is; it is what we make of it. Everyone "constructs" his own reality. We live with the certainty that we perceive the world "objectively." Yet this fondly held belief has long been brought into question by more than just cognitive psychologists because human perception is highly selective and subjective. A simple but obvious example: Yesterday evening, you decided to buy a new car made by brand X. The only thing you still haven't made the final decision on is the color. On your way to the office this morning, you see brand X cars everywhere and silently compare the colors. Did the number of brand X cars on the road increase phenomenally overnight? Surely not. You just didn't notice them yesterday.

Fallible Perception

Another example of the unreliability of our supposedly "objective" perception is offered by a film often shown in presentations: Two teams of five throw balls to each other. One team wears black T-shirts, the other white. The audience is asked to count along throughout the film clip how frequently the white team has ball contact. Most then watch with great concentration. Yet after the results of the count are compared by the group afterwards, the lecturer surprises them with the question, "Who saw the gorilla?" Anyone who hasn't seen the film before usually reacts with disbelief. And yet it is true. In the middle of the clip, a man in a gorilla suit walks through the frame, even looking directly into the camera. Hardly anyone in the audience sees him.[9] How is this possible?

---

9   You can also watch the clip on YouTube at http://www.youtube.com/watch?v=hwCzasHBXNc₁ (CRM BBALL Marketing FIN).

Perception Filters

The Brain as Filter

We would be subjected to constant sensory overload if our brains were not extremely selective. Every inhabitant of an industrial nation is confronted with approximately 2,000 advertisements daily, and that is only a tiny percentage of what we see and hear during a perfectly ordinary day. In order for us to remain capable of action with this glut of stimuli and information, our brains are equipped with an astonishing skill. The brain selects, evaluates, and processes all incoming information before it reaches our consciousness. The first and completely decisive step in the brain's pre-processing is the perception filters. Comparable with a spam filter, the brain discards a large portion of all information and stimuli received as irrelevant. We then do not perceive this information (consciously). But the problem with a spam filter is that information that is important for us often gets caught as well. The same thing happens with our perception.

Types of Filters

Perception filters can be divided into roughly three categories:

- Biological filters: We only see a certain part of the light spectrum. We only hear a certain range of sound waves, and our sensitivity is also restricted to a certain area.
- Filters of previous experience: Our perception is influenced by previous experiences, events, training, and knowledge. An architect perceives an old city center differently than a police officer, and an award-winning chef judges a restaurant differently than a fast food fan. Someone who has already lost a job due to bankruptcy registers warning signs that completely bypass a less-experienced colleague.
- Filter of interest: We only see what we want to see. Those among you not interested in fashion will take little note of what people wear (aside from extreme cases or particularly strong signals). That is why many men just shrug their shoulders helplessly when the day after a party someone says, "Ms. Smith was dressed very elegantly."

Distortions: Information Changed

Distortions are the processes of perception in which the original meaning of the information is changed. A piece of information is given either an inappropriately high or low level of importance. The most well-known examples might be "talking something up" or, conversely, "putting something down." Even many irrational fears can be traced back to distortions. A persecution mania is an extreme example of this phenomenon. In contrast, one of the most positive distortions of perception is falling in love: two people are sitting at a bus stop in the rain in a bad part of the city, and it is the most beautiful place in the world for them. (The brain really has to work hard sometimes.) But we do more than just ignore the dirt, concrete, and incessant rain to concentrate instead on love. Sometimes we also ignore worrying sales numbers or a slump in turnover. Anyone sitting there under pressure, hoping that things will be OK, will be tempted to find some "proof" that things really are about to take a turn for the better—even when it looks to outsiders like he is losing touch with reality.

Additions

Repairs in the Brain

If it doesn't fit, use a bigger hammer. The human "perception processor" strives for consistency; therefore, we strive for inner logic, coherence, and structure. On occasion, information arrives that is incomplete or incoherent. If these inconsistencies are big enough, they reach our conscious mind. Often, though, we don't notice a thing, or we try to remember, "What was that again?" The brain switches on something like an "auto-repair function" that repairs or eliminates the ambiguities. This function apparently has the perfect pieces available when, for example, you have not listened properly for a moment. Letters or words that are (repeatedly) missing in a text are added in this way. What is more, we can construct a meaningful message from alphabet soup without any problems. Or do you actually have trouble understanding the following text?

Aoccdrnig to rscheearch form an Elingsh uinervtisy, it deosn't mttaer waht oredr the ltteers in a wrod are in. The olny iprmoetnt tihng is taht the frist and lsat ltteers are in the rghit pclae. The rset can be a toatl mses and you can sitll raed it wouthit porbelm. Tihs is bcuseae we do not raed ervey lteter by itslef but the wrod as a wlohe. *

*Here is the text with correct spelling:

According to research from an English university, it doesn't matter what order the letters in a word are in. The only important thing is that the first and last letters are in the right place. The rest can be a total mess and you can still read it without problem. This is because we do not read every letter by itself but the word as a whole.

Real Information vs. Subjective Alterations

Our brain is particularly creative when connections appear to be illogical. Here the brain goes so far as to invent completely new information. This function often serves us well in our everyday lives. It has only one severe catch: the brain does not mark what it has changed or added. So we cannot distinguish between real information and subjective alterations and would swear on our mother's soul that something happened one way and not the other. Police officers who compare eyewitness accounts of the same incident can tell you a thing or two about this. It is quite likely that three witnesses of the same event depict it in three different ways. We experience similar things in our daily lives when we "process" family conflicts after the fact, for instance. Different parties almost always have very different versions of the events in mind. The question, equally beloved and fruitless, of how everything started (or who started it) usually cannot be answered.

Generalization

The Power of the First Impression

Once we have formed an opinion, then it tends to be self-confirming and to superimpose itself on new information, even if the new pieces of information contradict it. One form of this generalization is the effect of the first impression. Even if new or different information arrives that might put things in a different light, the first impression has a long-lasting effect that determines our attitude and hence actions. If one, for example, has decided to consider someone else competent and trustworthy, he will maintain this position for a long, long time—even if evidence to the contrary starts to pile up. This is one way that the inheritors of companies can be ruined by long-established managers; familiarity blinds them to the warning signals of wayward management until it is too late. One only needs to think of Madeleine Schickedanz and her bad luck with the selection of managers for the Karstadt-Quelle group, one of Germany's biggest department store chains, which was forced into bankruptcy.

Differing Worlds Are Possible

If one considers all these factors together, then it becomes clear that something like "objective reality" cannot exist. Perception—and with it perforce that which we consider "reality"—is highly selective and subjective. Paul Watzlawick elucidates this with a joke in which one lab rat says to the other: "I've trained this man so that he gives me food every time I press this lever."[10] In their world, they are actually right. Doesn't all the evidence point that way? In daily life, we will occasionally say that someone lives in another world. This is actually true to a greater extent than we realize. Our "worlds" fortunately coincide because we share similar previous experiences, knowledge, and interests, but every world alone remains an individual construction; we cannot turn off our perception filters. Is it still surprising that some managers optimistically work towards insolvency, even when the alarm bells are already sounding for everyone around?

ANTI-CRASH FORMULA

Do not (always) trust your eyes and ears! Regularly compare your view of the situation with others' view: managers, employees, maybe even outsiders (coaches and consultants). Make yourself aware of your own experiences and interests. To what extent do they influence your analysis of the situation?

---

10   Paul Watzlawick, *How Real Is Real?* (Munich: Piper, 2007), 81.

Stress, Perception, and Communication

Changes in Perception under Stress

So our perception is already highly unreliable in "normal" situations. But what happens when we are under stress? We have already heard from the accident researcher Rüdiger Trimpop that people in thorny situations concentrate even more strongly on small slices of reality and overlook everything from the cyclist on the one-way street to the airplane crash on the radar screen. In Crew Resource Management, the following changes in perception in stress situations are assumed:

- Perception is limited
- People develop tunnel vision
- Tunnel vision leads to stress-related distortion of perception

Fuel Emergency Results in Crash: New York, 1990

At the same time the manner of communication shifts (i.e., there is less communication, the tendency towards silent interpretation of others' actions grows), inhibitions for verbal attacks on others sink. For instance, a typical example for an air accident caused by poor communication is the crash of a Boeing 707 belonging to the Columbian airline Avianca near John F. Kennedy Airport, New York, in January 1990. There was bad weather on the US East Coast with fog and heavy winds. This is why the plane, which had taken off from Medellin, was directed into endless holding patterns and only received permission to land at Kennedy airport after a 90-minute delay. They had enough fuel for the flight to New York, as well as two additional hours of flight time. Unfortunately, their first attempt to land was unsuccessful; the pilot had to abort due to strong crosswinds and lost more valuable time—and fuel. Ultimately one engine after another failed, and the plane crashed off Long Island. Seventy-three of the 158 passengers lost their lives. The rest survived because there was no fire: the tanks were empty.

Communication Problems in the Cockpit

The science journalist Malcolm Gladwell, who looked at this example in his book *Outliers*, was astounded by the crew's passivity while catastrophe drew ever closer. "Through it all, the cockpit was filled with a heavy silence."[11] In a series of misunderstandings, the co-pilot was not able to make it clear to air traffic control at Kennedy Airport how desperate the situation was. The simple word "emergency" did not cross his lips. Instead, he remained satisfied with a comparatively weak, "We need priority." He noted, "We have hardly any fuel left." Because that is the case with almost all aircraft before landing, no one in the tower realized the dramatic nature of the situation.[12] If you read the record of the cockpit exchanges, you get the impression that, at some point, the co-pilot simply gave up. Cultural barriers came on top of that, which clearly made it difficult for the South Americans to speak bluntly to US air traffic control, who aren't known for their good manners.

Intellectual Emergency Procedures

Withdrawal and resignation; mistrust and negative accusations; paralysis and passivity; a stubborn insistence on a path started; being a "maverick," with little coordination within the team—these are typical types of reactions in stress situations and are well known in Crew Resource Management. Think about the last crisis situation in your company. Can you notice parallels? What happens when sales slump, careers are threatened, and drastic cuts are announced? How does that affect communication within the team? How differentiated are the arguments? How much planning goes into the reaction? How soberly is the situation analyzed? In his book about the management of complexity, the business psychologist Franz Reither diagnoses a tendency towards resorting to "intellectual emergency measures" in uncertain situations in which failure looms. He includes "avoidance reactions, sidestepping, downplaying, irrationality, resignation, premature reaction, oversimplification, diminished self-control, and solutions involving violence."[13] There it is again: the unholy trinity of running away, attacking, or playing dead, which our ancestors used to confront threats in time immemorial. But what might have worked wonderfully for the Neanderthals can lead directly to insolvency in the high-rise offices and production centers of today. What can you do to manage stress professionally in your company?

---

11   Malcolm Gladwell, *Outliers* (Frankfurt: Campus, 2008), 188.
12   Ibid., 193–194, and Waterkeyn, 157.
13   Reither, 113.

ANTI-CRASH FORMULA

Avoid speechlessness, isolation, and resignation. Demand and cultivate conversations within your team. Listen, even if you do not like what you hear.

PROFESSIONAL STRESS MANAGEMENT IN BUSINESS

A Winning Team: Stress Prevention and Planning for Emergencies

How well prepared is your company for critical situations? Even well-trained employees, rigorous oversight, and regular coordination and meetings on management level cannot prevent an organization from going into a tailspin. How can you keep problems from escalating till panic spreads? The best stress management is stress prevention. And once a crisis has arrived, you should have an emergency plan ready.

Crisis Simulation: Preparation for an Emergency

Insufficient Crisis Prevention Training for Managers

Training in a flight simulator is part of every pilot's training, and even later on, airline pilots will regularly have to test their skills and their "crisis resilience" in a simulator. Whoever has gone through stressful situations beforehand can act more rationally in an emergency. This is also the rationale for the training principles of elite police units and the military. Stress not only results from external stressors, but also from the interplay between a situation and individual perception. Why aren't there any "crisis simulators" in manager training? The approximately 30,000 company insolvencies in Germany every year should be reason enough to think about potential dangers, even if everything is running well at the moment.

Keep Possible Worst-Case Scenarios in Mind

If you want to avoid running around like a headless chicken if the worst should happen, you need to be prepared. That is why it pays to go through worst-case scenarios beforehand: What would be the worst possible development you could be confronted with in the foreseeable future? More concretely, could it be the loss of one of your most important clients, who makes up more than a third of your sales? Could it be the cheap products from a foreign competitor, who can deliver to conditions you cannot match? There could be a change in consumer habits that leads to a drastic slump in sales of your previously best-selling product. Prevailing tastes could change, or your product could garner negative headlines—never mind the reason. Your bank could cancel your line of credit, or your financing could fall through. Take the time and work out as many potential threat scenarios as possible. Watch out for downplaying techniques like, "Oh, that can't happen anyway." Go through the emergency situation concretely: how would you act? Why not devote one day a year away from normal business with the management team to plan for the worst-case scenario?

ANTI-CRASH FORMULA

Train for the worse case in a crisis simulator—at least for one day, once a year.

Crisis Simulation as an Opportunity

It is possible that concerns and fears for which there is no space in daily business will find voice in the preparation and carrying out of such a simulation. And it is very likely that you will learn about possible dangers from the discussion. Besides which, concrete ideas for everyday business will also emerge, whether you develop ideas of how to reduce your dependence on a key client and position yourself more broadly or appoint someone from marketing as trend scout, who from now on will carefully follow consumer habits. For example, what would happen if Junghans had regularly interviewed a mere 20 watch buyers of various ages about their preferences and reasons for purchasing? What if KfW had role-played extreme losses both in the main banking operation and at its subsidiaries—at the latest after the first signs of crisis had appeared on the financial market horizon? Possibly the policies of sticking one's head in the sand and paralysis could have been avoided.

Possible Results of Crisis Simulation

"What would happen if?" "How would you react in an emergency situation?" "What concrete steps would you take?" These are simple, as well as fruitful, questions that every company should pose regularly. It is much easier to plan rationally for difficult situations when times are good than if you are already up to your neck in water, and panic is spreading. In addition, such a role-playing game, even if only organized once per year, gives natural human inertia and the feeling of security we like to cocoon ourselves in a healthy kick up the backside. Furthermore, by thinking through the unthinkable, it loses part of its horror. At the end of such a crisis-strategy session, there should be a firm "emergency plan" that concretely articulates countermeasures and makes it easier to act rationally—even if worst comes to worst. Naturally, the loss of an important client is a threatening scenario, for me just as much as anyone. That is why there is a plan of action in my desk drawer, with concrete and considered steps to acquire new clients; it's a plan I will put into place the moment one of my key clients disappears.

ANTI-CRASH FORMULA

Develop emergency plans and checklists for possible disruptions to your business. Examine and update these lists and plans regularly.

Installing Alarm Systems: The Perception of Critical Factors

Install Warning Systems

In every cockpit, there are numerous visual and acoustic signals that inform the crew about technical malfunctions, critical limit values, and problematic flight situations. If the corresponding warning sound had functioned, then the Spanair crew probably would have noticed their fatal mistake (not extending the flaps) in time. Which "warning lights" exist in your company? Which warning lights have you defined for yourself?

Develop Early Warning Systems

Of course, internal statistics and record keeping fulfill such warning functions to a certain extent. Yet exploding costs, slumping sales, or reduced profits are frequently the consequence of mistakes that occurred much earlier. That is why your company or your department will ideally have an additional "early warning system." In contrast to the standardized sequences in an airplane cockpit, there is not a comprehensive system for the complex and differentiated situations in business enterprises that you can order as a finished product and have installed. However, it is possible to learn from risky situations in the past.

Developing an Early Warning System Step by Step

1. Think about when you personally have made mistakes that could have easily cost you your head. Ask the following questions:
    *   What mistakes were made?
    *   Can I recognize a pattern?
    *   Which factors or which stressors have to come together to cause this pattern again? Write these factors down.
2. Also consider the following questions and write the factors and circumstances for each:
    *   When were decisions made in your department that were, when viewed rationally, unsuitable, excessive, or hasty, and therefore were made when "not using your head" in the truest sense of the word?
    *   Which factors have to come together so that the company or the team can lose its head in that way, ultimately enabling such a mistake?
3. Can these factors reoccur? How high is the likelihood that your team will react to this trigger with the same pattern of behavior? Identify the trigger. Analyze and describe the neuralgic factors as precisely as possible.
4. Determine the early indicators for the occurrence of these factors, and set up an alarm system. Does your alarm system work? The best warning light does not help if the bulb is broken!

ANTI-CRASH FORMULA

Learn from the past: Which situations led to severe mistakes? How great is the danger that these mistakes will be repeated? Install an early warning system—and make sure that the light works!

Avoid Unnecessary Time Pressure

There are departments in which important tasks are always finished at the last minute: the preparation of the important annual trade fair, the gathering of quarterly numbers, or the delivery of a new product. However, small- and large-scale breakdowns regularly occur at this point, up to organizational worst-case scenarios. (You only have to think of the forgotten trade fair registration noted above.) Time pressure is preprogrammed weeks in advance as one of the most important stressors and often begins with small delays that add up more and more. For example, in one company in the confectionary industry, there is always a great back and forth between the marketing department and management about the packaging of a new product before launch. The packaging (as well as the product itself) is subjected to exhaustive consumer tests. However, that does not prevent bigwigs in the higher echelons from happily continuing to muse on whether the candy wrapper shouldn't perhaps have one more stripe after all. And couldn't they make the bag just a little bit more colorful? The subsequent punctual delivery of the product across Europe demands permanent crisis management. Warning systems based on time factors would no more be able to prevent this than systems based on organizational factors; at the third meeting on the packaging at the latest, old patterns of behavior will have set in once again!

Establishing a Standard Procedure: Acting Rationally

Do Not Panic

The most unfavorable things that can happen in a critical situation are wild, unconsidered panic reactions, which prove to be counterproductive and only make the situation worse. One example from aviation is the August 2005 crash of a Caribbean Airlines plane flying from Panama City to Fort de France on Martinique. Both engines had already failed. Even in this extreme situation, a commercial airliner is still capable of flying; it becomes a glider and could perform an emergency landing if an appropriate runway is within reach. Yet it seems the pilots clutched their controls in panic, trying to keep the aircraft in the air, instead of pushing the yoke forward, which would cause the nose to sink and thus increase the airspeed and, with it, the uplift.[14] The reflex of panic reaction (we're crashing! → pull up the nose) has led to crashes in other cases.

---

14 Waterkeyn, 157.

Kill Your Speed: Slow Down

In contrast to flying, in business it is extremely uncommon for split seconds to decide between life and death. That is why it is almost always possible to choose an option that aviators like to revert to whenever they can: the go-around. Abort the landing? Just do another round before you make a hasty decision. If you really "go around the block" or sleep over the matter and then call the team together the next day to search for the solution, the effect is the same: no wild, panicked reactions. Conscious deceleration is one of the most effective measures against rash reactions under stress.

ANTI-CRASH FORMULA

Stop your spontaneous impulse to act! Do you really have to decide and act now? Do a go-around rather than rushing into a mistake.

The Advantages of Checklists

It has long been recognized in aviation that all critical phases of a flight have to be worked through with a meticulous checklist. This approach is absolutely necessary, even with maneuvers that sometimes have to be carried out several times daily—especially with these, in fact. Checklists contain the respective firmly established SOPs, the standard operating procedures, for each process. If that process documentation reminds you of quality management frameworks, then you're not far off. Unfortunately, by now TQM (total quality management) has gained a reputation with many of being a useless "data cemetery," in which even trifles are documented in great detail and then disappear into the filing system, never to be seen again. This may be true for individual operating procedures in companies. But KfW Bank might have avoided getting so much egg on its face if it had ensured that money transfers over a certain sum be subject to a checklist that included checking the status of the receiver. It's a relief that standardized procedures are also defined and worked through by lists in the fields of pharmaceutical production and food production, or when you change your winter tires.

In every cockpit, there is a checklist for both normal and special procedures. The Spanair crew in the first example clearly skipped this checklist because it was, after all, "only" a routine operation. What checklists do you have in your company? It is highly recommended to set up SOPs, especially for the sensitive areas previously mentioned, where severe mistakes and problems in the company could emerge. Every error analysis should lead to a corresponding "preventative" checklist and ideally form short instructions, even emergency plans, for calculable emergency cases. Use checklists—especially in exceptional situations—and stick to them!

ANTI-CRASH FORMULA

Set your SOPs for operating processes where small mistakes could have big consequences. Formulate corresponding checklists.

STRESS—AND WHAT YOU CAN DO

ANTI-CRASH FORMULAS AT A GLANCE

1. Ask yourself occasionally, especially in the difficult situation, "Who's in charge right now: brainstem or cerebrum?"
2. Don't (always) trust your eyes and ears! Regularly compare your view of the situation with others' view: managers, employees, maybe even outsiders (coaches and consultants). Make yourself aware of your own experiences and interests. To what extent do they influence your analysis of the situation?
3. Avoid speechlessness, isolation, and resignation. Demand and cultivate conversations within your team. Listen, even if you don't like what you hear.
4. Train for the worse case in a crisis simulator—at least for one day, once a year!
5. Develop emergency plans and checklists for possible disruptions to your business. Examine and update these lists and plans regularly.
6. Learn from the past: Which situations led to severe mistakes? How great is the danger that these mistakes will be repeated? Install an early warning system—and make sure that the light works!

7. Stop your spontaneous impulse to act! Do you really have to decide and act now? Do a go-around rather than rushing into a mistake.

8. Set your SOPs for operating processes where small mistakes could have big consequences. Formulate corresponding checklists.

CHAPTER 2

WHO IS CRAZY ENOUGH
TO CRITICIZE A CAPTAIN?

(Or When the Boss Is the Problem)

+ + + February 6, 1996, Dominican Republic + + + A
Birgenair Boeing 757 crashes into the Atlantic Ocean
26 kilometers from Puerto Plata Airport. + + + 189 dead

The magazine *Der Spiegel* considered it the greatest
catastrophe in the history of German charter flights[15]:
an aircraft belonging to the Turkish airline Birgenair
crashes into the sea near the coast of the Dominican
Republic less than five minutes after takeoff. All
passengers die. Most of them are Germans on their way
back to Berlin and Frankfurt.

---

15 "Angst über den Wolken: Der Absturz der Boeing 757 vor Puerto Plata" (Fear above the
    Clouds: The Crash of Boeing 757 at Puerto Plata), *Der Spiegel*, 2001, www.spiegel.de.

The cause of this accident is a broken airspeed indicator. An airplane has three independently functioning airspeed indicators. The captain's gauge malfunctions and indicates excessive speed as they are cruising. Everyone is aware of this. In order to reduce speed, the autopilot raises the nose. The indicator continues to increase while the plane becomes slower and slower. The captain is still pulling up when the plane is almost vertical. The co-pilot and flight engineer both scream: "Don't pull up; push down!" Their instruments work. But neither of them have the courage to take the controls away from the captain. And the captain only trusts himself and his gauges.

AUTHORITARIAN LEADERSHIP AS A CAUSE OF INSOLVENCY

"The boss is always right!"? Actually, this model should belong to the past. Almost every manager claims to cultivate a leadership style based on partnership and emphasizes that his employees can come to him at any time. But how many employees actually dare to contradict their superiors in an emergency situation? When it comes to it, most of us are rather reserved. And although this is understandable, it does not always end well as managers are by no means infallible. Insolvency administrators name management mistakes as the most frequent cause of company failure. In a survey conducted by the University of Mannheim's Center for Insolvency and Reorganization (ZIS), "authoritarian, rigid leadership" was explicitly highlighted, along with "failures in oversight" and "financing gaps."[16]

CRASH EXAMPLE: PUERTO PLATA, FEBRUARY 1996

Unlucky Coincidences Pile Up

How can an experienced pilot make such a terrible mistake, blithely piloting his plane towards a certain crash? The starting point for the catastrophe was—as so

---

16 "Ursachen von Insolvenzen" (Reasons of Insolvencies), study by the ZIS on behalf of the Euler Hermes Kreditversicherung, www.wirschaft-kokret.de/de/insolvenzursachen/insolvenzursachen.html.

often it is—a chain of several unfortunate chance events. The flight was originally supposed to be carried out by a plane belonging to Alas Nacionales. However, due to a technical problem, the Boeing 757 from Birgenair was used instead. This plane had been sitting around on the apron of Puerto Plata's Gregorio Luperón Airport for around three weeks. Right at the commencement of takeoff, as the co-pilot made the routine announcement that a speed of 80 knots had been reached, it became clear that the captain's airspeed indicator displayed incorrect values. They still proceeded with takeoff—after all, there were still two intact airspeed indicators on board. Afterwards, investigators concluded that a pitot tube attached to the fuselage had been clogged, probably by dust or insects. Pitot tubes measure the pressure of airflow, making it possible to calculate airspeed during flight. If the probe is clogged, the gauge reacts to changing air pressure within the system. At some point, you will probably have seen red "remove before flight" tags attached to planes on the ground. With these tags the probes should actually have been covered and marked—standard procedure if an aircraft is left outside, to prevent the probes from being contaminated. It is obvious that, in this case, somebody did not do his job. Another unfortunate chance.

Uncooperative Management Style Proves Disastrous

Thanks to the lowered air pressure after takeoff, the pilot's airspeed indicator started working after all. Although the instrument was clearly malfunctioning and displaying wildly exaggerated airspeed values, the captain relied on his gauge (ignoring the other two) and activated the autopilot. The autopilot functioned perfectly. Unfortunately, it reacted to the (incorrect) airspeed measurement and tried to slow the supposedly too-fast plane. The result: the nose of the aircraft was raised higher and higher; the engines were cut back; the plane became slower and slower. At some point the "stick shaker" activated, and the control column started vibrating, warning the pilots that a stall was imminent. At this point, there could be absolutely no doubt the plane was flying too slowly. But the crew still did not take any countermeasures. Vital seconds were wasted; the plane ultimately crashed into the ocean. This did not occur because one of the pitot tubes was clogged. Rather, the cause lay in the fact that the captain did not want to hand over control and only trusted himself and his instruments.

CRASH WARNING

Every hierarchy needs functioning systems that control the manager.

COMPANY EXAMPLE: JÜRGEN SCHREMPP AND HIS WORLD, INC.— BILLIONS IN LOSSES FOR DAIMLERCHRYSLER

DaimlerChrysler: Hope and Reality

Journalists were already smugly asking in 2001, "How trustworthy is a manager who, during a merger, announced that he will create the most profitable automobile company in the world only to have to register a halving in profits two years later?"[17] They were referring to Jürgen Schrempp, CEO of DaimlerChrysler. Swabia, Germany's Black Forest region, known for its prudent business values, had become too small for Schrempp; he had set the ambitious goal of expanding the automobile builder Daimler into a global company. To achieve his aim, he initiated a merger with Chrysler in 1998 and invested more than €2 billion in Mitsubishi in 2000. Sheer size would then protect Daimler from being taken over. Synergies were intended to lower expensive development costs. But not everything ran according to plan: the stock value of the company shrank by 26 billion DM between 1998 and 2000; profits fell from 12.2 to 6.8 billion DM. Both Chrysler and Mitsubishi posted massive losses. In light of this situation, two *Spiegel* reporters asked Schrempp if he had ever considered stepping down. Schrempp leaned back and laughed, "Can you really see that happening? Someone like me?" They would need to throw him out: "If someone is in a position to change the captain—okay, then it will be done."[18]

Rapid Decline

Even at DaimlerChrysler, it took a long time for someone to stand up to "Captain" Jürgen Schrempp. In 2001 Chrysler had €5.3 billion in losses. DaimlerChrysler itself registered a €622 million loss.[19] The downward trend continued, and

---

17 Dietmar Hawranek and Dirk Kurbjuweit, "Die Drei-Welten-AG" (The Three Worlds Corporation), *Der Spiegel*, no. 9 (2001): 96.

18 Ibid.

19 "DaimlerChrysler: Chronik einer Auto-Ehe" (DaimlerChrysler: A Chronicle of a Automotive Marriage), *Focus*, February 14, 2007, www.focus.de.

stockholders repeatedly demanded Schrempp's resignation. But it was his internal critics who were shown the exit; for example, the head-in-waiting of the Mercedes-Benz Group, Dr. Wolfgang Bernhard, who had dared to express a contrary opinion to his mentor Schrempp at an April 2004 board meeting, was dismissed. Bernhard had thrown his weight behind criticisms voiced by some labor representatives and board members, and he spoke out for an end to the involvement with Mitsubishi. One week later, on April 29, the company officially announced that "Dr. Wolfgang Bernhard will not assume leadership of the Mercedes Group." That was exactly two days before Bernhard, the person upon whom the company's hopes had been pinned, was expected to take over.[20]

The "Captain" Departs (Too Late)

In contrast, the board extended Schrempp's contract up to 2008. However, he was only able to remain CEO till the end of 2005 before he was replaced by Dieter Zetsche. When the captain finally left the company ship, the stock market also breathed a sigh of relief: The day that Schrempp's resignation was announced, financial daily *Handelsblatt* noted an "impressive surge in the share price." At one point, the stock had gained more than 11 percent, reaching a level last seen almost three years before.[21] The rest is history. In 2007 the DaimlerChrysler divorce was finalized after less than ten years of marriage, and the majority of Chrysler was sold to the investment group Cerberus. It was the end of an expensive adventure for the Swabian company.

When the Patriarch Can't Give In

Can it be that some "office alphas" lose their grip on reality? Managers who choose a course and stick to it, come what may, regardless of how difficult it might prove to be and unheeding of colleagues' doubts, are not only to be encountered in huge multinationals. You all probably know some small- or mid-size business where an aging patriarch makes solitary decisions and leads his firm to the edge of the abyss. The ZIS researchers in Mannheim report the case of an 80-year-old at the helm of a family business producing machine tools who insisted on making every

---

20   Peter Brors, Christoph Hardt, and Carsten Herz, "Die letze Finte des Herrn der Welt AG" (The Last Feint of the World Corporation), *Wirtschaftswoche*, May 3, 2004, www.wiwo.de.

21   "Schrempp Rücktritt beflügelt Dax" (Schrempp Resignation Sparks DAX), *Handelsblatt*, July 28, 2005, www.handelsblatt.com.

decision himself. He set prices seemingly at random, as if he had been consulting an astrologer rather than sound financial data. As a result, equipment worth millions was sold for ruinously low prices, and the predictable end result was the company filing for bankruptcy. Up to the very end, management had only shrugged their shoulders helplessly.[22]

There is also the tragic case of Adolf Merckle. He founded pharmaceutical giant Ratiopharm—and took his own life in January 2009, after his empire collapsed. Months later, his son Philipp Daniel Merckle was to tell *Der Spiegel* that his father had created an "incomprehensible web of businesses" that was no longer manageable. The financial crisis had "only accelerated" the collapse. It is apparent that here, too, there was no diversity of opinion. According to his second son, the family that controlled the business was "ruled by a culture of silence."[23] Does that sound familiar? Even in stress situations (see chapter 1), the breakdown in communication was a factor that accelerated the crash. Companies might register bankruptcy due to poor results, but the real cause of the problem was their destructive communication culture, as we see again and again.

WHEN THE CAPTAIN IS SITTING AT THE CONTROLS

Division of Workload in the Cockpit

Regardless of which airline you fly with today, whether you board a plane in South America or in Europe, in the United States or in Kenya, there is a clear division of labor in the cockpit. There is a "pilot flying" (PF) and a "pilot not flying" (PNF). The PF flies the aircraft and makes all the main decisions; the PNF takes care of monitoring the instruments and providing general assistance, as well as operating the radio. These roles are not identical with that of the captain and the co-pilot—both can be PF as well as PNF. Cross your heart: as a passenger, who would you feel more comfortable having behind the controls, the experienced and highly trained captain or the relatively green co-pilot? Most passengers probably would choose the captain. Yet the accident statistics tell a quite different story; travelers should feel *reassured* when the less-experienced co-pilot is flying.

---

22 "Ursachen von Insolvenzen" (Reasons for Insolvencies), 22.
23 "Merckles Sohn fordert Rückkehr zu den Prinzipien ehrbarer Kaufleute" ("Merckle's Son Urges A Return to the Principles of Honorable Merchants), *Der Spiegel,* May 2, 2009, www.spiegel.de.

The Captain Paradox: More Experience = More Accidents

Is Experience Everything?

Airplanes are safer when the less-experienced pilot is flying. This is pretty surprising, since common sense tells us that experience is a reliable predictor of high-quality work. Whether he is our dentist, tax advisor, or handyman, we prefer to trust someone with more experience than a "greenhorn." Why doesn't this rule apply anymore in regard to the roles in the cockpit?

The Vital 5 Percent

Let us stop for a moment to think about what the essence of being a pilot really is. "Pilot" is commonly regarded as being one of the most stressful professions, comparable with air traffic controllers, paramedics, or prison guards.[24] According to my experience, that is only partly true: 95 percent of flying a modern airliner is pure routine, actually pretty boring, in fact.

These kinds of planes practically fly themselves. The pilot operates a few levers and presses a couple of buttons; it's less work than a bus driver does. Yet the other 5 percent of the time, the pilot has a hefty responsibility. If the routine is interrupted, if something unforeseen happens, if difficult conditions prevail, then pilots are suddenly under immense pressure. They are doing well if panic doesn't break out at this point. They are doing even better if they notice in time that the current situation is different than "business as usual" in the first place. The PNF is vital in this situation; he watches the instruments, gives important signals, and makes the designated "call-outs" in the context of the "standard operating procedures" (SOPs, cf. chapter 1). In short, the PNF is supporting and monitoring the pilot sitting at the controls. The PNF is even authorized (in fact, instructed) to take the controls out of the hands of the PF if he makes dangerous mistakes. The PNF will signal that with the command, "My aircraft," or "I have control!" Prize question: who has an easier time taking away the controls from the other, a captain or co-pilot?

Korean Airlines: The Problem Airline of the 1990s

It is not easy for an employee to contradict his boss. You won't need to explain that to anyone who has seen a company from the inside for more than a day or

---

24 http://arbeitsblaetter.stangl-taller.at/STRESS.

two. And at the same time, it does not matter if it concerns the production of automobile parts or pickles, or if we happen to be in a hospital or a factory. In an airliner cockpit, these inhibitions can have deadly consequences. And the greater the hesitation is, the more dangerous flying becomes. The story of Korean Airlines provides a strong argument for this thesis. During the 1980s and 1990s, it gained notoriety through a series of spectacular crashes; the science journalist Malcolm Gladwell calculated they recorded 17 times as many accidents as the US airline United between 1988 and 1998. In his book *Outliers*, Gladwell reconstructs several of them, from the near–shooting down of a 747 in Seoul, to the shooting down of a 707 in USSR airspace above the Barents Sea by Soviet fighter jets, to a 747 that smashed against a mountain on Guam, the largest of the Mariana Islands, in the early hours of August 6, 1997.[25] For a while, members of the US Army stationed in Korea were even forbidden to fly with Korean Airlines (today: Korean Air).

Aggravating Circumstances

Korean Airlines Flight 801, which crashed on Guam, killing 228 of 253 passengers on board, was also accompanied by the proverbial series of unfortunate events: the airport's instrument landing system (ILS) was not available that day due to maintenance; the Minimum Safe Altitude Warning (MSAW) was out of service due to a programming error. The ATC at Agana did not notice that the plane was flying much too low.[26] And yet, a former air force pilot with approximately 9,000 flight hours sat at the commands, had already flown to Guam eight times, and knew the terrain well. The plane was functioning perfectly. Well, what happened?

The Situation in the Cockpit

The captain had decided to carry out a visual approach. The advantage of this procedure is that the workload and length of flight path of an instrumental approach can be greatly reduced. But, as the name suggests, you need good visibility for this type of approach—of the ground below and of the runway ahead. The sky was cloudy, visibility was poor, and it was raining. The plane

---

25 Gladwell, 181.
26 Waterkeyn, 149–150.

broke through the bank of clouds for a moment, and the crew saw lights in the distance, which they thought were the airport. Yet even when the plane was only 500 feet above the ground, they still could not see a runway. Instead, the plane was headed towards the flank of Nimitz Hill, a mountain directly in their flight path. The voice recorder recorded the confusion of the crew. "Not in sight?" said the co-pilot, and the flight engineer uttered a surprised, "Huh." Vital seconds pass; the co-pilot suggests aborting the landing: "Let's make a missed approach." If he had intervened at this point and taken over the controls, then a crash would probably have been avoided, according to the investigation report. But he did not do it. The flight engineer repeats, "Not in sight." Followed by the co-pilot once again: "Not in sight, missed approach." The flight engineer: "Go around." Finally the captain also said, "Go around." But it was already too late; three seconds later, the collision occurs. Almost a half-minute passed between the first tentative warnings by the co-pilot and the flight engineer and the order to abort, with the plane heading towards the hill the whole time. The co-pilot had realized that they had lost their bearings. But he did not intervene. Clearly, he preferred to put his life on the line.[27]

Korean Good Manners . . .

Today, Korean Air is considered one of the safest airlines in the world. What has changed? It is simple: the Korean flight engineers and co-pilots have systematically learned to raise their voice, even when their superior is flying the plane. They were trained to change their communication habits. Where they previously restricted themselves to polite hints and suggestions, they now express themselves clearly and unequivocally. Set, unambiguous formulas are a fundamental part of Crew Resource Management. One example: in light of the poor visibility during the approach to Guam, the flight engineer cautiously said to the captain, "The weather radar has been very helpful today."[28] What he actually meant was probably more like, "In light of this weather, we shouldn't fly visually, but rather make a safe approach using instruments." But the pilot flying did not understand that. No one understands cautious hints if he is tired and stressed—or if he is asking himself where the darn runway is.

---

27 Gladwell, 205.
28 Gladwell, 205.

... And Western Good Manners

It is no coincidence that the comprehensive training Korean Air has required for all crew members since 2000 is carried out by a Western training agency. The Korean pilots of the doomed Flight 801 were basically victims of their national culture, which is characterized by finely differentiated hierarchies, extreme politeness, and an indirect, hedged form of communication. But what leads to a perfectly structured interaction in general society proved to be devastating in the plane cockpit. The considerate overlooking of lapses and mistakes is dangerous in crisis situations, and polite hints contain a high level of risk. Throughout the Western world, communication is much more direct (of course with differences), and the regimenting power of hierarchies is weaker. In particular, the individualistic cultures such as the North American, in which everyone has the right (and therefore almost the duty) to make one's own way, make it easier to talk plainly with each other. It is very hard to image an American co-pilot preferring to risk sacrificing his life rather than contradict his boss. One could, therefore, say that the Koreans learned to act more "Western" in the cockpit.

The Concept of "Power Distance"

In this context, Gladwell refers to the concept of "power distance," which the Dutch business psychologist Geert Hofstede developed on the basis of comprehensive international studies about the characteristic dimensions of a culture (others are individualism versus collectivism and risk embrace versus uncertainty avoidance). The greater the power distance in a society, the greater the respect towards authorities and the greater the inhibitions to risk a conflict with someone that is hierarchically superior.[29] It is hardly surprising that scientists were able to establish a statistical correlation between higher power distance between pilot and co-pilot and the number of airplane crashes. The more authoritarian and hierarchical the relationship in the cockpit, the greater the danger of a crash.[30]

---

29   Geert Hofstede, "Lokales Denken, globales Handeln: Interkulturelle Zusammenarbeit und globales Management" (Think Locally, Act Globally: Intercultural Collaboration and Global Management), (Munich: Beck-dtv, 2009).
30   L. Helmreich and Ashleigh Merritt, "Culture in the Cockpit: Do Hofstede's Dimensions Replicate?" Quoted in Gladwell, 186 and 262.

Increasing Complexity in the Cockpit and in Management

Flying surely has not become easier in the nearly twenty years that have passed since the crash on Guam, even if (and precisely because) the flight electronics have become increasingly capable and complex and take over more and more of the pilot's work. "We have already reached the limit of what a human can process in the cockpit, especially visually," said airline psychologist Reiner Kemmler, and "Today's pilots have to know more, plan better, follow the system better, and think ahead."[31] Isn't that strikingly reminiscent of the role of the manager in a globalized and increasingly complex economy? Just as pilots no longer operate control surfaces directly through the joystick, with manual control over everything, neither is it possible for managers in most businesses to have total oversight and control over their departments. In both cases, it is good if there are strong authorities that can support the person at the controls and correct him if necessary.

ANTI-CRASH FORMULA

Caution: If the captain himself is sitting at the controls, then the danger of crashing is greater, because the co-pilot is less likely to speak up. If you insist on taking the controls yourself, then at least make sure you have a co-pilot who contradicts you.

When Bosses Can't Let Go

Is Experience Always a Good Thing?

My flight instructor always said, "Experience is the sum of all survived mistakes." However, anyone who looks more closely at air accidents unavoidably begins to view the "experience" factor with mixed feelings. On the one hand, practical experience certainly does make you more competent, steadier, and more assured. The more experienced among us generally judge more quickly and accurately. They can compare the current situation with previous similar situations and draw the appropriate conclusions. It is likely that they have already made one or two mistakes and can avoid making the same mistakes again. To that extent,

---

31   "Der Stress beginnt am Boden" (The Stress Begins on the Ground), *Der Spiegel*,
     no. 31 (2009): 112.

experience really does make one smart. Yet, on the other hand, experience also appears to be able to make people "dumb and blind"—or at least careless. What if the situational comparison does not fit? What if your judgment and your conclusions are not right? The pilot of the Korean Airlines flight had already landed at the airport in Guam eight times before, and he was sure he could find the runway "again." It had always been there and had to appear at any second—a fatal miscalculation. Instead, he flew at about 250 kilometers per hour towards a hill only five kilometers away.

Carelessness as a Result of Experience

It seems that, the more often something goes off without a hitch, the more careless we become. This effect is not limited to airplane cockpits; think of the investment bankers in the international banking metropolises. They felt like "Masters of the Universe," even when they, aided by clueless investors, had speculated the world economy to the edge of the abyss. "Masters of the Universe": would it even be possible to encapsulate your own hubris and recklessness any more tellingly? This carelessness of "It's never been a problem before" is so widespread that we will dedicate an entire chapter to it (see chapter 3: "Landing in Bad Weather").

ANTI-CRASH FORMULA

Experience simultaneously makes you smart and dumb. Smart, because one can draw on comparable situations and act based on that experience. And dumb, because sometimes those comparisons can send us heading in the completely wrong direction.

Misplaced Managers

Another side effect of this "experience-related" hubris is the belief that you can do "it" best yourself. This belief causes superiors to intrude into operative business, even if they are actually responsible for oversight, control, and planning. One of my clients is a small, initially very successful, company that produces and installs steel structures. The boss helped with installation, even after the company had grown larger. The result: he got lost in detail and overlooked important decisions for the future; he neglected, for instance, decisions in the areas of organization, marketing, and the acquisition of new customers. By the time those responsible realized, it was almost too late. Supply bottlenecks and bureaucratic chaos had scared away many customers. Even here, no one had intervened internally, even though the difficulties could hardly be overlooked—quite similar to the Turkish captain or the Korean co-pilot.

Preferring to Get Lost in the Details, Rather Than Seeing the Big Picture

Wide-ranging experience is utilized much more effectively when it is not suffocated in the quagmire of details. In particular, those who have learned the business "from the bottom up" and know it "like the back of their hand" often have difficulties with a change in roles to a more measuring observation and planning position. Many continue to flee willingly into the depths of operative detail. This does not just apply to the heads of small family businesses. I know the CEO of a large mid-size company who, thanks to his engineering training, has remained an enthusiastic lifelong tinkerer. Doing the rounds through the company, he regularly startled his development engineers with concrete tips. No one dared to contradict him, and some ideas were only pursued because they "came from above," even if time had long since passed them by. However, here, as well, in the hard-fought mechanical engineering market, there were plenty of strategic tasks that needed doing. Instead of engrossing himself in the development of a new plug connector, the CEO should have kept an eye on whether his engineers' work was going in the right general direction.

The Valuable PNF Role

Such a flight into "favorite tasks" is not that uncommon. Just look around at your colleagues or circle of acquaintances. You probably know a lawyer who, as a CEO, prefers to meddle in his legal department; or a personnel expert who cannot deny his weakness for personnel management, even when he is already leading the entire company; or an IT expert who likes to program, even as the head of a large IT consultancy, instead of planning budgets and acquiring clients. At the same time, aviation teaches us, you are valuable as PNF, "pilot not flying"! It is good if you can contribute with your experience, but not by overreaching in operational activities. The optimal solution is to oversee the operational activities and only intervene in true emergencies.

POWER DISTANCE AND COMPANY SUCCESS

What Is the Leadership Culture in Your Company?

Cooperative Leadership: The Theory . . .

With a complex task, it is good when more than one is listened to. That is the way you might interpret results from the cockpit. Most work tasks today are complex. Of course, it is better if not just one person decides everything, and everyone else is downgraded to the role of extra or a mere cog in the machine. This isn't so new, you say? Hasn't authoritarian leadership been frowned upon for a good while now? That may be true. Theoretically, all leadership nowadays is "cooperative" (at least that is what you will hear if you ask that question in a job interview). Yet what does it look like in practice?

. . . And Practice

At meetings in your company, how often does anyone *really* challenge the boss's position? How often does an employee venture to express concerns, at least in a private conversation? Let us not kid ourselves; many people's trust in their superior's actual willingness to cooperate is muted. As a reminder, at its core, "cooperative management" means that superiors have an open ear for the ideas and suggestions of their employees and systematically consider their opinions in important questions before making a decision. (In contrast to the cockpit, companies are fortunate in rarely having to make decisions within minutes or even seconds.) Therefore, cooperative leadership has nothing to do with establishing democratic majorities and absolutely nothing to do with unguided laissez-faire. A cooperative approach is also reasonable because, as competent as he might be, no manager today can know everything, and because, in this way, an executive can benefit most from the competence of the team (to say nothing of the motivating effect for the employees of their voices being heard).

The Consequences of Authoritarian Leadership

The negative results of authoritarian leadership are well known. Thomas Gordon described them in his book *Leadership Effectiveness Training* over thirty years ago. Since then, the book has gone through countless editions. Some of the consequences identified by Gordon include the following: resistance, defiance, resentment, lying, cheating, submission, conformity, apple polishing, withdrawing, escaping, lack of creativity, and fear of trying something new.[32] It is no coincidence that this is reminiscent of the atmosphere at school, when the feared "strict" teacher laid down the law. Most of the pupils "hid" in class, waiting impatiently for the recess bell; a couple of bolder students rebelled, provoking the teacher and risking getting in trouble; and finally, a small group of teacher's pets tried to ingratiate themselves, giving the appearance, at least, of being totally fascinated by their domineering teacher's every word. A business department in which communication happens along these lines isn't exactly what you would wish for in a manager in the competitive world of the twenty-first century.

The Results of Inflexible Management

And yet the criticism of authoritarian attitudes is necessary even today. Barbara Kellerman, leadership expert and Harvard professor, wrote a book, *Bad Leadership*, identifying seven different varieties. One, along with incompetence, corruption, etc., is "inflexible leadership." She names former US Secretary of Defense Donald Rumsfeld as an example: "He certainly wasn't an idiot and by no means incompetent, but he was incapable of learning from his mistakes and accepting new ideas."[33] What are the consequences of such an attitude? The employees are afraid to voice criticisms or even make suggestions, and they hesitate to talk straight with their boss when there are problems. This "avoidance behavior" can be observed on the executive floors of many companies. There, employees are told that they cannot say this or that to the

---

32 Thomas Gordon, *Leadership Effectiveness Training* (Munich: Heyne, 1999), 25.
33 Steffen Heuer, "Ritterspiele" (Knights' Games), *Brand eins*, no. 4 (2009): 65.

boss "right now"—just as if the bearer of bad news would be beheaded, even today. Or can you imagine someone marching coolly into Jürgen Schrempp's office (or Ferdinand Piech's, or Hartmuth Mehdorn's, etc.) and calmly saying, "Boss, we have a problem. We've really messed up." If you just grinned, then your trust in an open communication culture—the prerequisite of "cooperative leadership"—cannot be that strong. It was this very cautious hesitance on the part of "subordinates" that cost Korean Airlines one plane after another and cost many people their lives.

Authoritarian Leadership: A Question of Age?

Of course, you might question whether or not the behavior of the "big beasts" on the top floor is representative of the management style of middle managers who are 20 or 30 years younger and who grew up in a different era. These executives are often quick to pay lip service to cooperation in general, and in most cases, it is accompanied by genuine conviction.

Yet how much theory survives in practical day-to-day management, particularly when things are not running smoothly?

Behavior of Leaders in Situations of Varying Difficulty

The mathematician and business psychologist Franz Reither wanted to get to the bottom of this question. He examined the decision-making habits of approximately 5,700 managers during situations of "low," "medium," and "high" seriousness. The result: during calm business situations ("low seriousness"), the majority of the managers surprisingly acted with more determination and more "brutally," in fact, than in "medium" situations—probably in an effort to inject some new vigor into the company. However, their reactions are even more drastic in difficult business situations. Typical here are behavioral patterns "that aim to deal with problematic situations in difficult circumstances (by which we are not talking about true crises or disasters) with a half-hearted attempt at a moderate intervention, and then turning more or less instantly to the 'overkill' approach . . . Rolling their sleeves up and getting stuck in" or even the tendency to apply "violent measures" appears to be characteristic for these situations. Reither's summary: "Handling complicated problems, there is a tendency to act dominantly. Unwanted developments are attacked head-on. They attempt to explain and control the entire situation exclusively according to their own preconceived ideas."[34]

The Consequences of Unilateral Decision Making

Simply put, people "act" cooperatively, but when the going gets tough, suddenly it is "no more Mr. Nice Guy." In politics, people like to talk about "putting their foot down." And, in fact, it is precisely in troubled times that it becomes clear how great the power imbalance is in a department. Those who use an authoritarian management style when under pressure can hardly be surprised when employees then prefer to keep their counsel when things return to normal. At the same time, those who tend towards unilateral decision making and powering through in an authoritarian manner when under pressure are taking an objective, factually verifiable risk. It is as if a plane starts to get into difficulties at 35,000 feet, with warning lights flashing and alarms sounding, and the pilot turns to the PNF and says, "Shut up and mind your own damn business!"

ANTI-CRASH FORMULA

Especially in difficult situations, there is a great temptation to "put one's foot down." But it always pays to get your coworkers' opinions before you make a decision, and now more than ever.

Why Employees Have to Be "Trained" to Speak Up

The Milgram Experiment

In the cockpit, the PNF is trained to observe the pilot flying and even take over the controls, if necessary. In everyday life, most people are more used to obeying authority. You may well have heard about the Milgram experiment in this context. In a spectacular experiment in the early 1960s, the American psychologist Stanley Milgram had volunteers "punish" another participant with electric shocks if he made mistakes when carrying out a task (word association). At the same time, the intensity of the (purported) shocks was slowly increased. The volunteers were told the focus of the experiment was about learning processes, but in reality, it was

---

34   Reither, 62, 67.

the extent of their belief in authority that was under scrutiny: how far are people willing to go when given orders by an authority figure?

The Power of Authority Figures

The sobering result: only a minority of the volunteers abandoned the experiment— even though, by the end, the participants they were "punishing" (in reality, these were actors) were writhing in pain and screaming, before collapsing apathetically in their chairs. As long as the "experimenter" told them to continue, the majority complied without objection—even to the maximum strength of 450 volts. The shocking thing is, these were volunteers; they had absolutely nothing to fear if they refused to follow instructions. What hold did the "experimenter" conducting the experiment have over them, these random people he had found through small ads in the newspaper? Now, think about what is at stake in the relationship between employees and management.

Neurological Causes

It is clearly very difficult to challenge authority figures. Most people are very reluctant to risk conflict. The latest neurological research supports Milgram's findings. From the neurological perspective, social conflicts are a significant stress factor that can interfere with rational action. In his book *The Biology of Fear*, the renowned neurobiologist Gerald Hüther wrote, "In all socially organized mammals, and with humans in particular, psycho-social conflict is the most significant and frequent cause for the activation of stress reactions that can easily become uncontrollable." He continued, "Individuals who lack a well-developed repertoire of social behavioral (coping) strategies are particularly badly affected."[35] Here is a simple example taken from my work as a consultant. A human resources manager has been looking at a new training methodology. Finally, she presents it to the CEO. He has no criticisms, but simply says, "What exactly can a trainer from outside the company do that our own people can't?" Instead of just answering the question (or passing it on to me), she immediately canceled the project. One does not necessarily have to call this "anticipatory obedience," and yet, the mere *possibility* of having to face some difficult questions is often enough to precipitate

---

35   Hüther, 43. Here "coping" means processing or adaption.

withdrawal. This is pure conflict avoidance and an indicator of high power distance in the company.

The Statistical Evidence: Germans Want Authoritarian Managers

This is why I doubt that the tendency to conflict avoidance and a preference for submitting to authorities has undergone any kind of fundamental change in the last forty years. In the summer of 2007, the Munich-based GEVA Institute published the results of an employee survey which consulted more than 11,000 people from different companies in 25 countries. According to the study, 41 percent of the Germans questioned agreed with the statement: "A manager should give employees clear instructions and not be influenced by differing opinions or outside events." And 80 percent even believed that managers should be "decisive and assertive." The institute gave the press release the following title: "Germans Love Strong Bosses."[36] It seems that a lot of people like working for "alpha" bosses who give clear directions (and, with that, relieve us of the weight of responsibility?).

Typical Leadership Myths

But that means that the dangers of blind faith in leaders do not just exist in cultures with an unusually high power distance (like in the Korean culture). The psychologist Oswald Neuberger puts something that can be observed often in daily life in a larger context. As soon as a superior starts to throw his weight around, cautious restraint spreads among employees, and hardly anyone dares to make even a quiet objection. In his standard work *Lead and Let Lead*, Neuberger refers to typical leadership myths. Upon closer inspection, in the day-to-day workings of the corporate world, they lead to a kind of moral cowardice, or at least a belief that "the boss will fix it." Myths offer orientation and justification in ambiguous situations. At the same time, hidden desires are articulated through them. Neuberger names a number of beliefs and attitudes among the leadership myths, including these:

- "This is a rational approach."
- "Everything is possible."

---

36   www.geva-institut.de. Fewer people desire authoritarian bosses in Sweden, for example. Only 17 percent of the Swedes believe that a superior should give "clear instructions" and "not let themselves be influenced by different ideas."

- "The cream rises to the top."
- "The manager has everything under control."
- "The goal is success."[37]

Workers' Opinions: Expressly Desired

Beliefs like these foster the conviction of the omnipotence of the man or woman at the top, and not only in the heads of the employees. The business press also enthusiastically helps construct this myth; for example, for years, Wiedeking was glorified as the "Savior of Porsche," while Apple founder Steve Jobs was lauded as a "visionary," and Helmut Reitzle, head of chemicals giant Linde, was praised as a "great strategist." If heroes, previously mythicized, fail to live up to expectations (anymore), then the disappointment is all the greater. One only has to think of Wiedeking. For the average worker, this can all easily culminate in a resigned shrug of the shoulders: "The boss knows what he's doing," even if warning signs are already starting to mount. And that would mean that the corrective "second opinion," which forms a key part of the safety system in all airplane cockpits, is absent from most companies. A company that wants its employees to express their views of the situation and openly voice their concerns and doubts has to expressly encourage them to do so. And above all, the manager has to avoid the cardinal sin of reacting too harshly when someone actually has the courage to speak his mind.

ANTI-CRASH FORMULA

Make sure your employees become self-confident, critical co-pilots—not disinterested underlings.

The Leadership Dilemma: A "Captain's Decision" and Being Able to Listen

Making Unpopular Decisions

A good leader listens to employees' arguments and then makes a well-informed decision that takes into consideration what he has heard. This is the best way to utilize the capabilities of everyone in your department and is also the best way to

---

37 Oswald Neuberger, *Führen und führen lassen* (Stuttgart: Lucius and Lucius, 2002), 100.

get each employee to buy in to your decisions and get behind them. That all sounds great, but unfortunately, it is no more than a half-truth. In the course of his career, almost every manager will have forced decisions through, against the opposition of employees. Anyone who has to cut budgets or let workers go is hardly going to be able to count on the creative support of his employees. Even those who merely want to change those familiar little rituals that form over the years will suddenly find themselves confronted by stonewall opposition. Anyone who has had to announce plans to switch to new computer software will know what I am talking about.

Chesley Sullenberger's "Captain's Decision"

In aviation, the courage to make clear decisions and defend them, even against possible resistance, is referred to as a "captain's decision." Chesley B. Sullenberger, who made an emergency landing with a fully occupied Airbus A320 on the Hudson River in the middle of New York in January 2009, made one such decision, and by doing so, saved the lives of all 155 people on board. The aircraft had collided with a flock of geese immediately after taking off from LaGuardia Airport, causing both engines to fail. The plane didn't have enough velocity to reach an alternative airport or return to LaGuardia. It proved fortunate that Sullenberger had more than 40 years of flight experience and, as founder and CEO of Safety Reliability Methods, had specialized in the behavior of pilots in crisis situations. It all ended well, so Sullenberger, is celebrated as the "Hero on the Hudson" to this day.

But what if it had gone wrong? What if the plane had broken apart upon impact or had even clipped the New York skyscrapers before that? It is almost certain that critical "experts" would soon have been found who would have told the world how "irresponsibly" Sullenberger had acted and just what a terrible risk he had taken.

When Immediate Action Is Needed: In the Cockpit . . .

Of course, you could counter that Sullenberger had no other option than an emergency landing on the Hudson because a return to the airport was impossible, and there was no other area free for an emergency landing in range. There was something else that was special about Captain Sullenberger's actions; he made the decision to land on the Hudson without hesitation. He probably knew his plan was risky. But instead of wavering and thinking about the consequences in the case of failure, he used every second to make the best approach to the Hudson. Hesitation would surely have been deadly.

. . . Or in Management

The difference between Chesley Sullenberger and most managers is that only very rarely do they have to make far-reaching decisions within seconds. Of course, when your offices are on fire, you do not schedule a group session and calmly discuss what the best evacuation route might be. But those kinds of situations, in which something has to happen immediately—this very minute—in order to avoid catastrophe, are rather few and far between in a management career. The media manager and former CEO of the Premiere pay TV group Georg Kofler offered an example in an interview in 2008. When the Kirch Media empire filed for bankruptcy, it looked like Premiere would be dragged down with it. But even during the live broadcast of the press conference with an insolvency administrator and an insolvency managing director Kofler made a typical captain's decision: "In that moment, I circled my desk in my office twice, then I said to my press officer: 'Premiere denies claims.'"[38] Two minutes later, this message hit the rolling news ticker on the TV, leading journalists at the ongoing press conference to interrupt: "Yes, but you know that Premiere is denying it." Even Kofler, who was known as a jack of all trades, clearly viewed this as an absolutely exceptional situation.

Find the Golden Mean

That means *you* have to make the decision. And sometimes you also have to make unpopular or risky decisions. Rarely, you may have to make these decisions *immediately* and under extreme time pressure. Yet it is in the really difficult situations that managers tend to hide themselves away and take far-reaching decisions in private on their own (see Reither's findings about decision-making habits). Employees seldom see their bosses as little as in crisis situations, when managers tend to brood behind closed doors before emerging to present the bad news. In these kinds of situations, what, actually, would be the disadvantage of taking other opinions on board as well? Listening to other opinions is also sensible because—inevitably—every decision you make is limited by your own subjective (and selective) field of perception and experience. Managers who are said to have

---

38   Roger Rankel, *Sales Secrets* (Wiesbaden: Gabler, 2008), p. 173.

completely lost track of what was going on in their company, to have lost touch with reality even, should be more than a warning. It is still up to you whether you use your team's ideas and suggestions or not. At the end of the day, a good manager has to be able to make an executive decision, at the decisive moment, and see it through—even against opposition. From my point of view, you also have to be able to take other opinions into consideration in order to avoid tunnel vision and bad decisions. This potential contradiction can only be resolved through the willingness to listen.

ANTI-CRASH FORMULA

Don't use the "captain's decision" as a justification for autocratic arrogance. Before you make a captain's decision, think it through: Does this really have to be done immediately? Do you have all the information you need to make a truly informed choice?

COOPERATIVE LEADERSHIP IN PRACTICE

The Complexity of Today's Working Life

Academic experts as well as practitioners agree that complexity is characteristic of today's business world. The processes, the tasks, and the demands on every individual in a globally networked and highly specialized economy cannot be compared with that of 100, 50, or even 20 years ago, before the Internet and email caused a further acceleration in work life. Anyone leading a traditional manufacturing firm in the 1950s, in which the same tasks were constantly repeated on an assembly line, might have been able to retain an overview of "his shop" and content himself as a manager with authoritarian commands. Only in the rarest cases will anyone managing a company or department today claim to understand all the processes and procedures or be able to solve problems by pulling rank. Similarly, the pilot in the cockpit of a modern airplane is reliant on a competent partner. An expressly hierarchical mindset—a great power distance—in a company precludes productive cooperation. It prevents employees from contributing their own ideas and also occasionally expressing objections. "We're not paid to think" is the mindset this leads to. On occasion, this might be defensive posturing, designed to conceal a lack of initiative, but often it is an expression of genuine resignation in the face of hierarchy, perpetuated by a rigid division of responsibilities and obsession with status.

Creating Prerequisites: Reducing Power Distance

Google: An Example of a Flat Organization

Those who wish to prevent decisions (and mistakes) being made in isolation are advised to actually put "cooperative" leadership into practice and make sure that the "power distance" to the employees doesn't become too great. Here, flat hierarchies can help. If there are only two or three levels in a business, then it's easier to speak openly than in a Byzantine bureaucracy, complete with a plenitude of different pay grades and balkanized into jealously guarded personal territories. It is surely not by chance that innovative organizations like Google, which made it from a two-person start-up to one of the world's most successful companies within 20 years, rely on an open culture with low hierarchical hurdles even today: "We strive to maintain the open culture often associated with startups, in which everyone is a hands-on contributor and feels comfortable sharing ideas and opinions. In our weekly all-hands ('TGIF') meetings—not to mention over email or in the cafe—Googlers ask questions directly to Larry, Sergey, and other execs about any number of company issues. Our offices and cafes are designed to encourage interactions between Googlers within and across teams and to spark conversation about work as well as play."[39] Can you imagine an employee at a traditional German company subjecting a board member to a full-blooded tackle during a game of soccer?

Living Communication

However, what is just as important as organizational charts and titles is living communication. In this respect, the manager's personal style sets the tone for the department. This gives you a chance to exert a positive influence, even if you are not in the happy position of being able to rewrite the company org chart. Here are some concrete measures to create a better communication culture.

---

39 http://www.google.com/about/company/facts/culture.

Hints for a Better Communication Culture

- Develop the most important (and rarest) communication skill: good listening. Give your employees your full attention when they express substantive questions. Avoid hasty interpretations and interjections. Ask follow-up questions. In short, listen "actively" (as is taught at every management seminar today).

- Ask your employees what they think, and take their opinions seriously. Make sure there is a constructive climate in meetings. Prohibit personal attacks and unfair rhetoric by others.

- Observe yourself while communicating: Are you letting your employees finish their thoughts? Do you avoid reprimanding, embarrassing, or punishing critics after the fact? Think about your function as role model.

- Whoever wants information has to give information; so, no power games, no secretiveness. Be a fair communicator. If you can't say something about a certain topic right now, then let them know why.

- Approach your employees, and be interested in their opinions. That does not have to happen within the context of a meeting; check out the idea of "management by walking around."

- Explain your decisions, and avoid imperious power plays: "Just do what I say," "Because I want you to," and "Let other people do the thinking."

- Cultivate a culture of positive mistakes. Part of open communication is that mistakes can be made and that mistakes are treated constructively (see chapter 6: "Non-Punishment Reporting System"). Employees who are afraid to make mistakes are generally reluctant to express opinions and make suggestions.

- Develop your antennae. What is important is not only *what* is said, but *how* it is said. If in meetings you regularly encounter a wall of silence, crossed arms, sneers, or overzealous nodding, then you have lost your co-pilot.

ANTI-CRASH FORMULA

If you want to lead cooperatively, then you must communicate openly and fairly.

Avoiding Errors of Judgment: Ensuring a Corrective

In his book *The Situation Is Hopeless but Not Serious*, Paul Watzlawick tells a story that has become world-famous, the story of the man with the hammer:

> A man wants to hang a painting. He has nails, but no hammer. His neighbor does have one. Therefore, the man decides to go to him to borrow it. However, at that moment he begins to have doubts. Imagine that the neighbor does not want to lend me his hammer? Yesterday when he greeted me, he was also a bit short. Maybe he was in a hurry. Or maybe he was just pretending and he really has something against me. What then? I've never done anything to him; who does he think he is? If somebody wanted to borrow my tools, I would lend them to him right away. Why wouldn't he? People like that guy make your life miserable. And I'm sure he imagines that I am dependent on him, just because he has a hammer. That does it! The man storms over to the neighbor's door, rings the doorbell, but even before he has had a chance of saying "good morning," the man yells at him, "You can keep your hammer, you jerk!"[40]

Before you laugh at our quick-tempered friend here, consider for a moment how you yourself arrive at judgments and decisions. You recall impressions and experiences and draw your own conclusions. In turn, this line of reasoning determines your actions. If your life has been halfway successful, then your interpretations have clearly mostly overlapped with your environment. If not, then you must feel like the man with the hammer. The fact that your neighbors no longer talk to you will be the least of your problems.

Checks and Balances

What Watzlawick shows in his fantastical way is that we are all prisoners of our own experiences and interpretations. We "construct" our reality. And we have no choice because we cannot overcome the barriers of our own perception. Therefore, it is reasonable not to consider our own worldview as universal and infallible. Instead, we should actively seek out different points of view. In the everyday business context, a trustworthy and competent colleague or superior can be such

---

40   Paul Watzlawick, *The Situation is Hopeless but Not Serious* (Munich: Piper, 1984), 39.

a corrective, a sounding board who prevents you from getting carried away (and overlooking all the warning lights). If there is no one in your surroundings you trust, then an external sparring partner might be suitable, for instance, a coach. It is best if you are advised by someone who has both experience in business (leadership experience as well, if possible) and a psychological toolkit. A good coach won't tell you what you should do but will pose the right questions and in that way "help you to help yourself" in the best sense of the phrase. In a preliminary session, your coach will explain exactly what he intends to do and how he is going to go about it.

Evaluation Using 360-Degree Feedback

Many large companies emphasize the use of 360-degree surveys, above all to correct the blind spots in the self-perception of their managers. Everyone who works with a particular manager on a daily basis gives an anonymous "review": employees, superiors, clients, selected business partners. Some of those affected reject the 360-degree feedback as a hidden instrument of discipline and control, and occasionally it is, in fact, misused in this way. However, in almost all cases, you will receive nothing worse than helpful pointers for your own continuous personal development. You might even be made aware of characteristics you have that sometimes trip you up; for instance, the survey may pinpoint a tendency to unilateral decision making, poor coordination within the team, or even failure to make decisions promptly. Even surveys carried out only among employees can fulfill this goal. However, ideally you can communicate so openly with your employees that you do not need an extra questionnaire.

Ensure You Get a Good Mix

Of course, the culture in your department is strongly influenced by the people you surround yourself with. So the job interview stage is the time to make sure you are not just employing "low maintenance" yes men. The company and even you personally will profit from self-confident characters who also occasionally challenge you. And here is another obstacle you can avoid at the same time: the tendency to "stick to your own." There is a saying in America, "We like each other when we are like each other." This often produces a high level of sympathy right from the get-go, but in the long run, it leads to a staffing monoculture. People tend to take their eye off the ball when they are too busy admiring each other.

ANTI-CRASH FORMULA

If you never encounter any objections at work, you need to start worrying. Either you are infallible, or you have neglected to foster proper checks and balances.

Offering Frameworks for Discussions: Blogs and Comment Boxes

Lack of Options for Employees to Express Concerns

In any average hotel room there will be a customer feedback form; on the Internet, it is possible to get an overview within seconds about how tour operators, restaurants, or books are judged by others. As a trainer, I subject myself to an evaluation by my participants after every seminar. But in daily office life, there are only restricted opportunities for "users" to express their opinions. Those who can't bring themselves to express their opinion in an eye-to-eye conversation or in the weekly departmental meeting are effectively condemned to silence. Frustration then often finds an outlet through the office grapevine. Add to this the fact that if your company has a culture characterized by careful maneuvering and remaining close-lipped (or your department was led by a rather authoritarian predecessor), you will not be able to change the communication in your team overnight. Trust grows slowly, but dies in a moment.

Unwelcome Criticism

What's wrong with giving employees the option of "safe" (anonymous) expression of opinion, from simple comment boxes to a company blog? Large companies such as Siemens offered this possibility through their intranet. In Siemens's case, this took place at a time when the company was going through a difficult economic phase (2006, when mass layoffs were threatened and board members rather shortsightedly gave themselves a 30 percent pay raise). The company blog was used so enthusiastically that the magazine *Der Spiegel* online reported "Siemens Employees Revolt on the Internet." That was clearly more feedback than Siemens senior management cared for. It was officially announced that this was only a small minority of "disgruntled" workers.[41] The chance for communication unfortunately went unused. Whoever asks for opinions should handle them constructively. You can assume that you will not always like what you hear, and remember the charming expression: you can put lipstick on a pig, but it is still a pig.

ANTI-CRASH FORMULA

If your employees have difficulties with open dialogue, then lower the psychological hurdles by offering them opportunities to express themselves anonymously.

BAD COOPERATION—AND WHAT YOU CAN DO

Finally, to close out this chapter, all the measures you can use to avoid the captain's paradox, expressed once more.

ANTI-CRASH FORMULAS AT A GLANCE

1. Caution: If the captain himself is sitting at the controls, the danger of crashing is greater, because the co-pilot is less likely to speak up. If you insist on taking the controls yourself, then at least make sure you have a co-pilot who will contradict you.
2. Experience simultaneously makes you smart and dumb. Smart, because one can draw on comparable situations and act based on that experience. And dumb, because sometimes those comparisons can send us heading in completely the wrong direction.
3. As a manager, do your best as "pilot not flying." Keep the entire system in mind, and only intervene to correct worrying trends. Guard yourself from your "favorite tasks."
4. Especially in difficult situations there is a great temptation to "put one's foot down." But it always pays to get your coworkers' opinions before you make a decision, and now more than ever.

---

41   "Siemens-Mitarbeiter revoltieren im Internet," *Spiegel online*, September 26, 2006, http://www.spiegel.de/wirtschaft/30-prozent-mehr-fuer-vorstaende-siemens-mitarbeiter-revoltieren-im-intranet-a-439346.html.

5. Make sure your employees become self-confident, critical co-pilots—not disinterested underlings.

6. Don't use the "captain's decision" as a justification for autocratic arrogance. Before you make a captain's decision, think it through: Does this really have to be done immediately? Do you have all the information you need to make a truly informed choice?

7. If you want to lead cooperatively, then you must communicate openly and fairly.

8. If you never encounter any objections at work, you need to start worrying. Either you are infallible, or you have neglected to foster proper checks and balances.

9. If your employees have difficulties with open dialogue, then lower the psychological hurdles by offering them opportunities to express themselves anonymously.

CHAPTER 3

LANDING IN BAD WEATHER

(Or When a Target Becomes an Obsession)

+ + + November 24, 2001 + + + A Crossair Jumbolino
breaks up in a forest during its approach to Zurich
Kloten. + + + 24 deaths + + +

"Pilot responsible for Crossair crash," reported
the Swiss broadsheet *Neue Zürcher Zeitung* after the
publication of the official investigation in February
2004.[42] What had happened?

That November evening, a plane belonging to the
Swiss airline Crossair was flying from Berlin to
Zurich airport. Visibility was poor, hampered by low-
lying cloud cover and light snow. In the cockpit, the
flight crew were already looking to quitting time. The

---

42 "Pilot responsible for Crossair Crash near Bassersdorf," *Neue Züricher Zeitung*, February 3,
    2004, www.nzz.ch.

pilot, a flight instructor with almost 20,000 hours of experience, decided to take a visual approach, despite the poor weather conditions. During the approach, the aircraft dipped below certain minimum altitudes, and the pilots knew it. That is what the electronic warning systems are for. Although the ground could only fleetingly be glimpsed from between wisps of cloud, the captain continued the approach undeterred and hoped that the runway would become visible soon enough. It had worked out till that point. But this time is different. Suddenly there was a bang as the plane clipped the tops of several trees on the crest of a hill and crashed into a wooded valley. Twenty-four of 33 passengers and crew on board died.[43]

ARRIVALITIS: A FORM OF GOAL FIXATION

There is a sarcastic designation for what happened here: "arrivalitis"—hardly anything is as tempting as "almost" being at the destination. In these situations, even experienced pilots forget or ignore the usual safety measures and give in to the temptation of risky maneuvers; the Jumbolino crash is anything but an exception. In this context, experts speak of goal fixation: the rigid concentration on one current goal (here: landing now!) that pushes everything else into the background and leads to tunnel vision and carelessness. Does that sound familiar? When was the last time you said to yourself, "Close your eyes and say a prayer," in your everyday business life?

GERMAN CORPORATIONS: TOO HESITANT IN TIMES OF CRISIS

In some companies, people think like this till just before an economic crash. A mixture of "It'll be all right" and "It just *has* to work" leads them to ignore clear warning signs—or not even register them in the first place. In extreme cases, this goes on to the point of failure to register insolvency in time. In these cases, the same mix of goal fixation and risky maneuvers found in the Crossair crash have

---

43   Jan-Arwed Richter and Christian Wolf, *Mayday! Flug ins Unglück* (Munich: GeraMond Publishing, 2006), 131.

the upper hand. Studies prove that in difficult times, warning signals are ignored and countermeasures taken only with great reluctance. In the August 2007 issue of marketing magazine *Brand eins*, Tim Zimmermann, partner at strategy consultants Roland Berger, is quoted as follows: "Current surveys by Roland Berger demonstrate that it takes an average of 20 months before German companies initiate measures to fight a crisis. Only a third reacted within the first year (compared to 50 percent in the rest of Western Europe). And even then, German managers are quicker to consider redundancies as a reaction to a crisis than managers in other European countries, and fall back on classic financial resources such as loans, 'while new investors do not sufficiently make use of their position to steer a restructuring.'"[44] You might put it like this: first it is "close your eyes and say a prayer," and once the horse has already bolted, people react like headless chickens. This is all reason enough to take a closer look at the phenomenon of goal fixation and human reactions to risk.

CRASH EXAMPLE: ZURICH, NOVEMBER 2001

Zurich: Unfortunate Circumstances

A captain with almost 20,000 flight hours, who is doing a "visual approach" despite driving snow and heavy cloud cover, all the while dipping below the prescribed minimum altitude and who refuses to be "distracted" by warning systems: how can this be? The Crossair plane, an Avro RJ100, also known as a Jumbolino, had taken off from Berlin Tegel at 8 p.m. and started its descent towards Zurich Airport around 45 minutes later. During the descent, the crew was directed to a new runway. Due to noise abatement measures, they were not able to land on the designated runway 14, but now had to use the shorter runway 28, running east-to-west, after several rounds in the holding pattern. The pilot's reaction: "Oh, sh*t . . . that too, alright, ok."[45]

The First Landing Option: With the ILS System

In contrast to runway 14, on the newly designated runway, there was no instrument landing system (ILS), but only a so-called "non-precision approach" available.

---

44 Matthias Hannemann, "Good from experience," *Brand eins,* no. 8 (2007): 74-75.
45 Richter and Wolf, 132.

The difference between these two kinds of approaches is as follows: During the ILS approach, a precision approach, the pilots follow a guidance beam that leads them exactly to the runway threshold with great precision. In order to be able to follow this beam, two indicators are brought together in one special instrument. One gauge indicates the vertical deviation from the beam and thus shows if a plane is too high or too low. The second gauge depicts the horizontal deviation to the guide beam and thus shows whether you are to the left or the right of the guide beam. If both gauges are centered, then the plane is right on the ILS. The ILS is the safest and most reliable approach procedure and, for that reason, also the prevailing standard.

Second Landing Option: The "Non-Precision Approach"

However, there are also runways that are not equipped with ILS, for instance runway 28 at Zurich. In a "non-precision approach," there is a fixed point of navigation, for example, a beacon and a range finder that shows the distance to the fixed point. The approach works like going down stairs. Precisely established altitudes have to be maintained at precisely established points of distance. For instance, the beacon has to be flown over with at least 5,000 feet of elevation. Two miles after the beacon, you can descend to 4,000 feet, and after four miles to 3,000 feet, and so on. Although this procedure sounds somewhat complicated, it is practiced again and again by pilots and belongs to an aviator's standard repertoire. It is important that the plane's altitude never falls short of the minimum because it guarantees that there is adequate obstacle clearance. If you descend too early, it could be that there are things in your way you may not be able to see at times of poor visibility. And these objects are usually very hard. It would be interesting to know if the "Oh, sh*t" was in reference to the complicated approach to runway 28. It is possible that this outburst was simply the result of the two Swiss pilots wanting to clock off and get home.

Captain's Decision: Visual Landing

Both pilots prepared for the new approach. The 56-year-old captain knew Zurich airport and all approaches to all the runways very well. His junior colleague confirmed that he too knew the new approach well. Whatever guidance method they might have chosen, be it ILS or "non-precision," in light of the poor visibility, they surely should have used an instrument approach. To make matters worse, another Crossair plane that had just landed had reported that visibility on the ground was "near minimum"—they had only been able to see the runway at a distance of 2.2 miles. Yet the Jumbolino pilot decided to do it differently. He looked out the windshield and began with the descent. "Although the vague outline of the ground below them kept emerging, neither pilot was able to see the lights," writes Christian Wolf in his depiction of the accident.[46]

The plane continued to descend and repeatedly dipped below the prescribed minimum descent altitude. The pilots were also made aware of this through the "ground proximity warning system" (GPWS). In addition, the speed of descent was too high. The elevation of 1,000 feet is approximately 300 meters. Depending on weight, the approach speed of a passenger jet lies at around 140 knots, or about 155 miles per hour (250km/h). If you were moving through fog at this speed, you would want to be very certain that there was nothing in the way, wouldn't you? If there is even the slightest uncertainty, then there is only one course of action: go around!

Pilot's Delayed Reaction

All the while, the pilot muttered, almost imploringly: "24 [hundred feet], the minimum . . . I have [visual] ground contact . . . at the moment; we're continuing on . . . It's coming up; we have ground contact . . . We're continuing on . . ."[47] Ultimately the automatized voice of the radio altimeter reported that they were only 300 feet above the ground ("minimum, 300"). At a descent rate of 1,200 feet per minute, you only have 15 seconds till you hit the ground (not including trees in the calculation). Only then does the pilot, who still can't see the runway, decide to abort, after hesitating briefly. But just as he was starting the maneuver, there was a collision. The plane scraped some trees and crashed into a wooded area three miles from the airport. The airplane immediately caught fire. There were 24 casualties, including both pilots. Nine passengers survived the impact.

Crossair's Own Pilot Briefing

The ensuing investigation revealed a series of unfavorable circumstances: obstacles in the approach to runway 28 were not marked in the maps; the air traffic control

46   Ibid., 134.
47   Ibid.

was understaffed; the co-pilot was not even half the age of the captain and didn't dare to contradict his former flight instructor. Taken individually, however, these things do not lead to a crash. It has to come along with a pilot who systematically ignored the warning signals because he wanted to get home quickly and because he liked visual landings.[48] This was apparently encouraged by a lax safety culture at Crossair: "In the context of the investigation over 40 cases were uncovered from the years 1995 to 2001 in which the crew developed their own procedures or had not followed the rules of existing procedures,"[49] according to the official final report by the Aircraft Accident Investigation Bureau. In addition, the news platform Swissinfo circulated rumors about a strange hiring practices at Crossair: "According to the indictment, over an evening meal, Suter [founder and president of the board of directors] supposedly said to newly hired co-pilots that a good Crossair pilot could sink below the minimum safe altitude without problems—and would also be able to land despite poor visibility." This was reported at the commencement of the trial against the former manager.[50] This clearly worked out well for a while and led to a "close your eyes and say a prayer" mentality.

CRASH WARNING

Never "close your eyes and say a prayer"! Especially just before reaching the goal, keep your eyes open and stay fully concentrated. Be "go-around-minded" up till the very end—and be prepared to postpone a business transaction or a negotiation, for example.

COMPANY EXAMPLE: VOLKSWAGEN AND THE FORAY INTO LUXURY SEDANS

The Phaeton: The Luxury Product from VW

If you ever happen to be near Dresden, don't miss the chance to see a rather unusual attraction. Only a few tram stations from the historic city center is Volkswagen's

---

48   Christian Wolf tells of a "resistance to following the instruments while flying," ibid., 136.
49   Final report number 1793 from the Aircraft Accident Investigation Bureau, p. 84, www.bfu.admin.ch/common/pdf/1793_d.pdf.
50   "Ex Crossair "Spitze vor Strafgericht" (Management in Court), April 28, 2008, www.swissifo.ch.

transparent automobile plant. The German newspaper *Sueddeutsche Zeitung* mused that it is probably the "only automobile factory that has an air of nobility—with parquet flooring—almost somewhere you could live in."[51] The Phaeton has been built here since December 2001. The standard version of this fine automobile costs around €60,000 or $80,000; those purchasing various extras, from the most powerful engine to the "complete leather Volkswagen Individual 'Sensitive Classic Style' for front seats with 18-variant settings "[52] can add another €40,000 on top. You could afford a nice Porsche for this price.

No Success Story

The Phaeton is the pet project of the VW chairman, Ferdinand Piëch. His goal: pitting VW against the competition from southern Germany with its own full-sized luxury car to pull even with the BMW 7 Series and the Mercedes S-Class. The fact that there was already a full-sized luxury car being produced by the VW group, namely the Audi A8, was clearly of no interest to Piëch. The painstakingly manufactured Phaeton was expected to sell at a rate of 20,000 per year. However, for a while it was only 5,000.[53] In the United States, only 650 specimens were sold within nine months, leading Volkswagen to completely shelve their Phaeton experiment there in the summer of 2006.[54] One would think that might have been enough of a warning signal to rethink the project. But undeterred, VW production for Europe, even though the Phaeton was jeered by the car magazine *Auto Bild* as being "as rare as hens' teeth on our roads."[55] It's apparent even to laypeople that such a project can't possibly be profitable. The whole thing is a disaster from a business point of view, but to date no one at Volkswagen has even thought of ending the project. On the contrary, in the summer of 2014, there were plans for a new 2015 version. This, despite savage criticism in the press of "Piëch's luxury

---

51 Michael Kuntz, "Ferdinand Piëch und der Phaeton—Ein luxuriöses Hobby" (Ferdinand Piëch and the Phaeton –A Luxurious Hobby), *Süddeutsche Zeitung*, April 4, 2008; www.sueddeutsche.de.

52 www.volkswagen.de/vwcms/master_public/virtualmaster/de3/modelle/phaeton/zahlen_fakten/infomaterial_preise.html.

53 Thomas Hillenbrand, "60 Deutsche Autos—Der VW Phaeton" (60 German Cars —The VW Phaeton), *Der Spiegel* online, June 7, 2009, www.spiegel.de.

54 "VW Phaeton—Goodbye America," *Manager Magazin*, November 14, 2005, www.manager-magazin.de.

55 Quoted according to Hillenbrand, loc. cit.

hobby" (*Sueddeutsche Zeitung*) and warnings on the Internet of a "money-eating-machine" in light of the dramatic losses.

The Great Target Fixation at VW

What makes a sober person like Ferdinand Piëch hold firm to this expensive adventure for years on end? Target fixation seems to be the only reasonable explanation. The desire to charge forward with VW into the luxury class is clearly so great that everything that speaks against it is simply ignored. This obsession with "marching on" at all costs is fatally reminiscent of the Crossair pilots who continued their descent to reach the target, even though they couldn't see the runway. There was surely no shortage of warnings at Volkswagen. Any head of marketing who earned his job will have asked himself if the brand VW can radiate so much status and glamor that people hand over a six-figure sum for a VW product. Yet it is obvious that warning voices were ignored by the business "flight crew."

UMTS: Unexpected Revenue for the State

Target fixation is not limited to automobile producers: think for a moment of the auction of the UMTS mobile broadcast licenses in Germany in the summer of 2000, for instance, which brought in over €50 billion for the national coffers. The bidders—including all large mobile communications companies—drove the price up to dizzying heights. In the end, they each paid around €620 per German inhabitant to get a UMTS license at all costs. The Finance Minister at the time, Hans Eichel, rechristened UMTS as "Unexpected Monetary Transfer for Sovereign Debt."[56] Today the companies' actions are considered an "investment worst case scenario."[57]

Target Fixation: A Widespread Characteristic

But if we are honest, we all tend to occasionally have that "money's no object" attitude. Many people pile on debt till it is up to their necks in order to fulfill their dream of having their own house. The goal overshadows everything, makes them throw all caution into the wind (along with all the warnings from well-meaning friends) for dubious credit offers and then hope up to the foreclosure auction that

---

56 "Milliarden-Roulette um eine ungewisse Zukunft" (Billion Roulette to an Uncertain Future), *Manager Magazin*, July 27, 2000, www.manager-magazin.de.
57 www.flatrates-umts.de/allgemein/2010-versteigerung-von-umts-lizenzen-887.

it will "somehow work out." The same effect causes investors to throw good money after bad because they (want to) believe that "sure thing" stock tip will pay off in the end. Target fixation makes people careless and blind, and that makes it dangerous. What is behind it, and how can it be prevented?

IN LOVE WITH THE GOAL AND BLIND TO DANGER

Target Fixation: Fairy Tales and Reality

Goals have a good reputation, in business as well as with numerous success gurus. People lead towards targets, fix sales targets, and insist on clear project goals. Some enthusiastic cheerleaders go one step further and promise that you only have to believe in your goals to achieve them. Popular movies and bestsellers are always written according to this pattern; at the center are usually bold heroes who are able to turn around almost hopeless situations, precisely because they stubbornly hold on to their goals. Unfortunately, life is not pulp fiction. However, anyone who studies the topic of target fixation soon gets the feeling that many people believe such trivial myths in real life.

When a Target Becomes an Obsession

Cause for an Excessive Target Fixation

Let us note: setting goals and energetically striving towards them is generally considered a virtue—for good reason. However, when orientation towards a goal tips over into target fixation, then things become risky. Then people switch into an "at all costs" mode, neglecting alternative actions and overlooking clear dangers. Naturally, there is the interesting question of when and how clear-eyed orientation towards a goal turns into stubbornness and delusion. In this respect, there are two central factors of influence:

1. The closer and more tangible a goal appears, the greater the tendency to hold on to it. (Motto: "It will all work out in the end.")
2. The more people have already invested in reaching the goal, the stronger the resistance to giving up the goal. (Motto: "Close your eyes and say a prayer.")

Unconscious Strategies

However, the dumb thing about it is that insanity now feeds itself. The subconscious desperately tries to justify what it has created. Admitting to defeat or even a mistake is out of the question. People prefer to invent ludicrous explanations ("secondary rationalizations") to vindicate their behavior. Well, and if their actions are so well justified, why should they be changed?

The Catastrophe on Mount Everest

This isn't just the case in aviation, expensive product developments such as the Phaeton, or the purchase of dream mansions. The fatal mental mistakes that can lead to target fixation are also plain to see in mountain climbing. Petra Badge-Schaub, co-editor of the anthology *The Psychology of Safe Action in High-Risk Sectors*, takes a commercial Mount Everest ascent from 1996 as an impressive example.[58] At the time, two groups were making their way to the summit: one under the leadership of the New Zealander Rob Hall, the other led by the American Scott Fischer. In addition to the seven and eight Sherpas, respectively, and two leaders, each group had eight paying customers. The adventure ended with eight deaths and several severe injuries. Events unfolded with a series of absolutely unbelievable mistakes, especially on the part of Rob Hall, an experienced mountain climber. His group had started around midnight on May 9. Hall had previously determined 2:00 p.m. as a firm turn-around time, regardless of where they might find themselves. In mountain climbing, you not only want to get to the top but also safely come back down. The majority of mountaineering casualties happen on the way back. This is also a result of target fixation, which makes people throw caution into the wind; climbers want to reach the summit—even if they exceed their limits—and forget that they will no longer have the strength for the descent.

Irresponsible Actions of the Tour Leader

That is why it is a *very* good idea to establish a firm turn-around time for everyone. Yet the person who violated this was Rob Hall himself. He not only encouraged a client who was already thoroughly exhausted to carry on, without thinking about

---

58   Petra Badke-Schaub, Gesine Hofinger, and Kristina Lauche, *The Psychology of Safe Action in High-Risk Sectors* (Berlin: Springer, 2008), 113.

the way back, but he himself only reached the peak at 4:00 p.m. Encouraged by this example, Scott Fischer continued his ascent, although this meant his group had to turn around and continue without him. He would die, just as some of his customers would. In contrast, Rob Hall had convinced another client he had to leave behind to wait for him to come back. At the same time, he completely disregarded the fact that his own timely return was not at all assured. The man waited for ten hours and avoided freezing to death by a hair's breadth. Rob Hall sent a SOS to base camp because he couldn't bring the exhausted group members down by himself. Upon this call, a mountain climber went off to support him. The completely exhausted climber couldn't be saved, even with their combined efforts. And the rescuer also lost his life, not least because, by then, a snowstorm had blown in along with temperatures of −50°C. Rob Hall didn't make it down either; he died.[59]

An Inner Struggle

Try to picture the situation, if only approximately: You're just short of the peak. You have made 14 hours of extreme effort in icy temperatures. And now you're just supposed to give up? This demands almost superhuman self-control. It demands the sober calculation of possible secondary costs (here: death) against the massive emotional pull of the target (here: wanting to reach the summit). This level of circumspection is only achieved by very few people; rationality usually gets the short end of the stick. Instead, people ignore the risks, make careless mistakes to the very end, and convince themselves that it will all work out.

ANTI-CRASH FORMULA

The closer a goal appears to be, the more carelessness creeps in. Especially when the goal is in sight, keep a cool head.

Near Catastrophe in Vienna

Non-mountaineers are often astounded by mountain climbers' unwavering obsession with reaching the summit. Air travelers would be just as astonished

59 Jon Krakauer, *Into Thin Air: A Personal Account of the Mt. Everest Disaster* (New York: Anchor Books/Doubleday, 1999).

if they knew that thoroughly qualified and well-trained pilots have the same fixation with "arrivalitis." One further example: in July, 2000, two Hapag-Lloyd pilots made a crash landing at Vienna International Airport because they ran out of fuel on the way from Crete to Hannover. The reason: they weren't able to retract the landing gear of their Airbus A310, which led to excessive fuel consumption. The two pilots "forgot" this while calculating their fuel needs. The pilot's association Cockpit commented, "You don't even need an instruction manual for that, every beginner even knows that."[60] But that's not all; although the fuel gauge had already shown the fuel was almost gone by the time they were around Zagreb, the pilots kept on flying instead of immediately looking for a place to land. There was just one single system, the Flight Management System (FMS), suggesting the plane would make the distance. However, the FMS is programmed to assume that unusual flight behavior will only persist until the next waypoint. A waypoint is similar to an interstate exit. And because it's illogical to carry out an entire flight with the landing gear extended, this case doesn't exist in the FMS programing. Nevertheless, the fuel gauge indicated that there wouldn't be enough fuel. The fuel flow indicators, which indicate how much fuel is currently being used, showed that there wasn't enough fuel left. Everything pointed to there not being enough fuel. Now, relying completely on the FMS is about as reckless as setting off to cross the desert in a Jeep with the gas gauge already pointing to empty—just because your GPS told you it was "close enough!" Unbelievable, right? The 142 passengers escaped with nothing more than shock from the emergency landing.

How Can You Recognize Target Fixation?

Target Fixation Everywhere

As much as you might be shaking your head, no one is immune to the behavioral patterns described above. Numerous political projects have been forced through to a bitter conclusion that had clearly been on the horizon. Like the "health fund" given to state health insurance companies in Germany in 2009 to reduce costs—even though experts warned about a bureaucratic monster that would cause the

---

60 Tatjana Meier, "Piloten berechneten Kerosin-Verbrauch falsch" (Pilots Miscalculate Fuel Consumption), *Berliner Zeitung*, July 22, 2009, www.berlinonline.de.

opposite, driving up costs and paralyzing competition between the insurers. That's exactly what happened. Again, numerous students have continued to pursue an unloved course of study instead of putting the brakes on in time, following the maxim, "I've already been at it for so long." The result? Seventeen semesters and a career as a taxi driver.

A Textbook Example: The Music Data Bank

There are countless cases of companies continuing to develop products even when everything seems to indicate that costs are out of control and that the market demand just isn't there. A previous client of mine, a small company that had specialized in the area of software and media development, got into this kind of trouble a couple of years ago in an almost textbook way. The Internet was still in its toddler phase, so online-based networks were still wholly unknown. It was in this context that the idea of a comprehensive music databank formed. A computer program was supposed to gather all the information available about modern music, organize it, and make it searchable and organizable. Everyone in the company was enthusiastic about the idea, and at least in the beginning, there was a recognizable market for the product. Unfortunately, they were all overtaken by the technical developments. The Internet grew and developed. The benefits that their product (still far from being finished) would have offered to customers continuously shrank compared to free online competitors. But by now, the company was running on autopilot. They had invested so many resources and man hours in the project that there was no alternative to success. So they kept adding new features to the program, to keep it ahead of the Internet competition. Yet all the polish and new features they added to the program simply consumed more money and resources. By then, those responsible were completely resistant to advice. Every criticism was blocked—rather harshly in some cases. What shouldn't be, couldn't be.

You can imagine how that ended. Funds were exhausted. The banks revoked lines of credit. The databank was never finished, and the company no longer exists. When was the last time you thought, "We've already invested so much; we can't give up now"? An emergency landing might have saved the company, but, in such situations, most people clearly regard an emergency landing as a defeat.

ANTI-CRASH FORMULA

It is more courageous to make a controlled emergency landing in hazardous situations than to risk a crash landing. Emergency landings are unpleasant, but less deadly than crashes.

How can you recognize when people are no longer acting rationally and goal oriented, but rather in an obstinate and target-fixated way? Here are some indicators:

1. The desire to achieve a goal represses everything else and dominates people's thoughts. They "must" reach the goal—"whatever it takes."

2. The logic of the project is no longer questioned, even if the difficulties mount.

3. Killer arguments are used with increasing frequency. Critics are fired.

4. People avoid thinking about alternative actions and stubbornly remain on the path they have chosen.

5. The amount already invested is in everyone's thoughts. Badge-Schaub calls this the "justification of effort."[61] Unfortunately, this defense of previous investments and tasks is a fool's errand at a time when the company may be on the verge of failure.

6. Dangers are downplayed. ("Everything will work out." "It's all worked till now.") People accept risks that would never be considered under normal circumstances.

7. Those responsible hope that everything will go precisely according to plan—even though this is *never* the case in practice ("planning optimism").[62]

8. Perception is extremely selective. Consciously or unconsciously, people search for information that strengthens their own perspective. Counterexamples are downplayed—to the extent they are registered at all.

9. People comfort themselves that "the others" are also carrying on. Think for a moment about the silent Crossair co-pilot and the influence of Rob Hall as an unfortunate role model during the Mount Everest ascent. Or think

---

61 Petra Badke-Schaub and Eckart Frankenberger, *Management kritischer Situationen* (Management of Critical Situations) (Berlin: Springer, 2004), 91.

62 Ibid. 126.

about the last meeting of the department managers, where no one dared to question the "keep going!" mentality. In this context, researchers speak of the normative power of "groupthink," which leads competent individuals to make mistakes as a group.

Patterns of Behavior from Early Childhood

This all has an aura of wishful thinking. People resist taking possible dangers seriously or even considering alternative courses of action because the alternatives, in the short term at least, are less attractive than continuing with the preferred course of action. It is just nicer to fly straight back home rather than having to make a stopover and refuel. It is more attractive to carry on and reach the summit than to admit to yourself that you can't manage it and that you had better immediately turn around. And it is more pleasant to keep your mouth shut in a meeting than to attract the ire of the collected department managers. Psychologists would say that people are falling victim to the pleasure principle of early childhood, which we never quite manage to overcome: we want, if at all possible, to avoid pain and pursue pleasure, preferably without delay.

ANTI-CRASH FORMULA

Pay attention to your inner voice. Take it as a warning if phrases like "It has to work," "It'll be all right," "There's no alternative," and "Close your eyes and hope for the best" start being bandied about. They are a signal that it is probably time to pull the emergency brake and take a calm, considered look at everything.

THE HUMAN IRRATIONAL WAY OF DEALING WITH RISKS

What We Are Afraid Of

In 2009 people were afraid of the swine flu, in 2008 it was avian flu, and in 2001 it was mad cow disease (BSE). To date, none of these illnesses have caused nearly as many deaths in Europe as traffic accidents do every day. Judged by the reaction to BSE, the idea of having to get in the car in the morning should make our blood run cold. It is almost certain that more people have drowned in the bath than have died from bird flu. All of this makes us suspect that human handling of risk isn't exactly characterized by rationality.

Typical Characteristics of Risky Actions

How can it be that people worry about climate change and at the same time risk their health by smoking and eating fatty foods? Individual risk perception is curious, as psychologists know.

The Essence of Human Risk Behavior

- **We get used to risks.** We underestimate risks that we are exposed to daily (familiarity breeds contempt, after all) and become careless. One example: the perpetual struggle to maintain safety standards. Not only Crossair pilots are somehow careless. Gardeners poison themselves because they become careless in their handling of weed killers—not despite but precisely *because* they handle them daily.[63]

- **We consider voluntary risks less dangerous than risks imposed upon us.** One example: Countless investors sank their money into obscure investment vehicles or deposited it in an Icelandic bank (!) at the turn of the century.[64] Imagine if your bank manager tried to force you to do just that or they'd refuse to do any more business with you. You would probably switch banks immediately.

- **As long as we are capable of acting, we like to believe we have everything under control.** This is the reason why many more people are afraid of flying than are afraid of getting behind the steering wheel of a car—although, statistically speaking, the drive to the airport is the most dangerous thing about flying. Of course, people don't have everything under control when in traffic, not least because all the other drivers believe the same. That's why psychologists speak of a "control illusion": we consider risks we have no influence on (epidemics, radioactive waste, carcinoid substances in food, etc.) as subjectively more dangerous than many things more likely to cause accidents where we are actively involved (smoking, driving cars, alcohol consumption, etc.).

63 www.toxinfo.org/publiktionen/GizmuenchenJahresbericht2004_2005.pdf.
64 As the largest Icelandic Bank, the Kaupthing Bank was declared bankrupt by the Icelandic Financial Oversight Committee in October 2008.

- **We have difficulty imagining "it" could happen to us.** Cancer, heart attacks, firings, being shot down by our partner, running a business into the ground—everyone knows about these "life risks," yet in our own perception, these events affect other people, not us. This basically optimistic attitude naturally has its good sides and guards us from hypochondria or chronic jealousy. However, in times of crisis, it is dangerous because it lures us into the trap of selective perception.

The Importance of Risk Control

If you consider all these components of human risk handling all at once, then it's no longer surprising that experienced pilots take risks that can't be quantified and end up crash landing. Becoming used to the task, voluntary decisions, and the illusion of control—it all fits together. Pilots and managers are often convinced that a crash is something that only happens to others, at worst. We just aren't programmed to consider the possibility that we ourselves might make mistakes or meet with failure. An initial countermeasure consists in becoming aware of the irrationality of one's own risky behavior. Think about developing some sort of risk-control system. Keep assessing the risks you are actually taking, especially during everyday situations and procedures.

ANTI-CRASH FORMULA

Keep in mind the old aviation saying: "There are old pilots; there are bold pilots; yet there aren't many old, bold pilots." The difference between courage and boldness is small but dangerous.

Risks in Companies

The Dilemma: Realistically Assessing Risks and Opportunities

The fact that business wouldn't be possible without taking risks is one of the first things you learn in a business school textbook. Business activity is the same as betting on the future, and no one can predict it in detail. This is the foundation of the basic dilemma: every new business idea, every new project, involves risks as well as opportunities. How can one avoid overestimating the opportunities and underestimating the risks? Where is the border between irresponsible carelessness, energetic pragmatism, and excessive caution? Are there such things as positive characteristics in the first place?

Due Diligence: From Pedantry to Carelessness

In Crew Resource Management, airplane crews are sensitized to the fact that the healthy self-confidence that a conscientious pilot needs is the result of a precarious balance. Every characteristic is only positive and effective to a certain degree. If the quality or characteristic is too pronounced or too weak, then its effect is often reversed. Diligence is surely a sensible trait, whether flying a plane or leading a company or department. But we all know people who take being diligent too far. Then it becomes pedantry. On the other hand, too little diligence often leads to imprudence and carelessness. The basic goal is finding the perfect balance between insecurity and arrogance, between carelessness and pedantry.

Figure 1: Dimensions of attributes.

Adaptability Required

Extremes are dangerous. Prudence means finding the right balance between self-confidence and meticulousness. Unfortunately, this "right amount" is always changing. Our environment is constantly changing; the requirements are constantly changing. Therefore, what makes up sensible, effective action is always changing too. That means effective action always requires flexibility. This is necessary not only to bring an airplane safely back to land, but also to lead a company or a department or to complete any other demanding task successfully.

A Standout Example of Not Knowing the Risks

An example: I had been commissioned to coach an entrepreneur from the field of real estate. The client predominantly earned his money by purchasing real estate from foreclosure sales and insolvencies. Once the piece of real estate had been purchased, the goal was to renovate the building or at least find new renters. After a certain amount of time had passed, the client then sold the piece of real estate again, at a profit, of course. So far, so good. For a long time this businessman seemed to have the devil's own luck. He was especially successful in the period after German reunification. The more dealings I had with this client, the more I began to ask myself: does he really know what he's doing? Many of the properties were purchased with nearly no risk check at all, to say nothing of market analysis. As long as the market was booming, it worked like a charm. As long as enough people absolutely wanted to buy real estate, the risks weren't a factor, because the property was gone again much too quickly. I don't have to tell you that the market cooled very strongly at the beginning of the new century. The economic crisis caused my client massive problems. Suddenly he was stuck with his real estate. And all the risk factors he had previously ignored now took their revenge.

Human "Classes of Risk"

By nature, people have different levels of risk affinity. Every financial advisor knows to categorize his customers as either "risk-averse," "risk-neutral," or "risk-embracing" investors. Differing attitudes towards risk affect not only the way people handle money but also human activity in general. Some people enjoy extreme sports; others are happy playing golf. Some people regularly spend their monthly income down to the very last cent; others worry about their retirement funds until they are old and gray—despite having a secure job and an impressive bank balance. Even among entrepreneurs, there are risk takers and cautious, bank-manager types. People can lose their money through speculative investment or by letting changing times pass them by. Anyone who wants to avoid a crash should avoid both extremes.

Three Steps to a Better Handling of Risks

The first step towards the "perfect balance" is self-reflection: Which risk group do I belong to? Am I risk-averse, moderately careful, or more risk-friendly? A second step consists in ensuring that you have a good mix within your team, instead of surrounding yourself with people who share your own attitude towards risk. Ideally, the daring and cautious employees balance each other out. A third step is a functioning control system. In business schools, these have long been a matter of discussion, under the label "risk management."

Limits of an Alarm System

There is not enough space here to discuss this in detail. But this much should be said: risk management is most advanced in the area of banking, where credit and asset risks are fine-tuned with the help of sophisticated financial mathematical models. Ironically enough, all the financial mathematics in the world could not prevent the financial crisis. The heart of the matter is that the best alarm system is only as good as the people who use it. That is why even legally mandated reporting and monitoring obligations cannot prevent supervisory boards from failing and boardrooms from assuming risks that endanger the continued existence of the company. The best alarm is useless when people are determined to ignore all the warning signs. And as we observed with the example of Crossair, the tendency to ignore danger is greatest when an appealing goal is almost within reach: the generous bonus, the destination airport, or soaring sales figures. So what concrete steps can you take in your everyday business life, either to prudently reach your goals or abort in time?

ANTI-CRASH FORMULA

The best alarm system is useless when the warning signs are systematically ignored. Ensure that there are people surrounding you who take warning signs seriously. Establish a risk-control system.

PROFESSIONAL HANDLING OF GOALS AND RISKS IN A COMPANY

However tempting your target is, it is essential to keep your head. You need to keep your feet on the ground, even when you have almost reached your goal. Here are three concrete suggestions that will help you hold steady until the end: curb hubris and carelessness, maintain flexibility, and act prudently.

Curb Hubris and Carelessness: The Dark Side of Success

Great Wits Are Sure to Madness near Allied[65]

Maintaining an awareness of your own failings is one of the most difficult tasks in daily life, especially if you have become accustomed to success in the past and are regarded as an "old hand." In the previous chapter, we have already emphasized how experience can simultaneously make you dumb and smart. Smart, because you can assess situations better (and frequently also more reliably). And dumb, because the (self-)assurance acquired in this manner can lead to carelessness and hubris in the long run. So it is no coincidence when an experienced pilot flies through a snowstorm by sight and a less experienced pilot, who is more likely to think of the possibility of his own failure, uses his instruments. The longer someone has gone without making a mistake, the greater the chance he starts to feel invulnerable.

Case in Point: Porsche and VW

That dynamic might have led the Porsche CEO Wedelin Wiedeking, spoiled by success, to put all his eggs in one basket in the struggle with VW in 2009. He thought he could crown his years-long run of successes with the takeover of Europe's largest automobile concern, a company that was 15 times as large as Porsche. Wiedeking clung stubbornly to this plan till the very end and ultimately had to leave the company. The proud Porsche marque was integrated into the Volkswagen Group.

ANTI-CRASH FORMULA

The more enticing the goal is, the more (self-)critical you should be, because the greater the likelihood that you won't want to perceive the dangers. Ask yourself to what extent you are truly ready to give up your project and turn around. Be honest with yourself.

---

65 Attributed to John Dryden, http://www.brainyquote.com/quotes/quotes/j/johndryden154237. html.

Causes of the Seveso Catastrophe

Success can make you arrogant, can even give you delusions of grandeur. It is fertile soil for risky habits and the disregard of safety precautions. Most accidents in the chemical industry appear to be connected to the attitude "It's always worked out," including the devastating catastrophe that occurred in the Italian city of Seveso in 1976. On July 10, highly poisonous dioxin gas escaped from chemical works run by Roche subsidiary Icmesa, contaminating a large area and injuring more than 400 people. Inadequate safety measures, untrained personnel, careless handling of poisonous vapors, and a chain of unfortunate circumstances led to the catastrophe. Jörg Sambeth, the former technical director of the plant and the only person who later apologized to the victims, made the following remark in an interview with the German daily newspaper *Taz* in 2006: "The accident occurred through sloppy work that day; that is true. But the real cause was crass mistakes made by management years before . . . and the plant had absolutely gone to the dogs."[66] With this backdrop, reports about "poisonous clouds of smoke" that "constantly collected under the roof," gain new credibility.[67] In most companies, thankfully, sloppy work usually results in legal disputes, delays, and substandard goods at worst; here, there were deaths and serious injuries.

Key Questions

The lesson is always to question what you are doing—especially when everything is going well:

- What are you doing differently than a year ago, two years ago, or even five years ago?
- Why have you changed your approach? What advantages does this bring?
- Are you paying for these advantages (perhaps saving a little time or money) with increased risk? What is the worst-case scenario of the new approach?
- Are there rules that are permanently broken in your company or department? Why? Are the rules bad, or is it possibly an attitude that has snuck in over the years?

---

66 "I Was Absolutely Stupid," *Taz*, July 10, 2006, www.taz.de.
67 "I Was Absolutely Stupid," *Taz*, July 10, 2006, www.taz.de.

ANTI-CRASH FORMULA

Regularly check your habits: What has been done differently recently and why? Which procedures have snuck in that, upon closer examination, harbor considerable risks?

Experience Does Not Preclude Failure

So if you have been successful for too long, then there is a danger that it will be *you* who provokes the next failure. Even real experts are not immune to this effect. In his piece "Behavior in Crisis Situations," Franz Reither wrote: "Coincidentally, errors can also be found among experienced and responsible experts, who have had high self-estimation on the basis of their previous achievements."[68] That should be warning enough to frequently and repeatedly question your own view of things.

Maintain Flexibility: The Use of Turning Points

Establish Turning Points

Especially when entering new business territory, it is sensible to define clear "turning points" in advance. In this way, you can avoid costs getting out of hand or the bent to unwaveringly pursue projects that are clearly heading towards failure. Unambiguous turning points are based on exact numbers: if you have not reached the summit of Mount Everest by 2:00 p.m., you turn around—regardless of where you happen to be. In aviation there is the so-called "missed approach point" (MAP), or the minimum descent altitude. This point is a precisely defined position at a certain altitude and a certain distance from the edge of the runway. If you have reached this point, then the runway must be in sight. If you do not see it, then you abort—always! An airplane is called an airplane because it is better at staying in the air than it is at landing. And a business is called a business because there is business to take care of. Otherwise, it would be called "neglecting" or "maintenance." So you need to define clear MAPs and halt lines for your business, project, or department— and stick to them. Vague declarations of intent are worthless. The criteria need to be clearly measureable. Here are a few examples.

---

68   Reither, 74.

Criteria for Turning Points

- What is the latest date at which you have to receive the first research results before making the decision to develop a product further or not?
- What is the maximum amount of money you are prepared to invest before you reassess or even cancel the project?
- How many pre-orders have to be received by day X before you can start production?
- Which or how many partners do you need to join you to make the project viable?
- How many sales does the project or service have to generate for it to remain viable? How many in the first year, the second, the medium term?

Choosing the Right Moment

This also means clear turning points have to be established *before* the project starts. This will prevent irrational behavior taking hold when you are already "in the air," trying to justify expenditure, for example. It's common to employ the sunk cost fallacy: "We've already invested so much; we can't turn back now!" What is hidden behind this "can't" is a purely emotional argument, not logic or reason. What happens in a moment like this is a mixture of wishful thinking and self-deception, which arises from the completely understandable hesitance to admit failure. In order to avoid becoming the victim of their own emotions in this way, prudent investors give their financial advisors clearly defined target prices at which they want to sell—and they stick to them! This method can prevent a manageable loss from becoming a catastrophic one.

Testing Alternative Scenarios

Turning points can mean turning around, suspending, or even abandoning a project. At the very least, they should be grounds for reevaluating a project and considering alternative scenarios:

- What is the hitch exactly? What is going differently than planned and why?
- Which conclusions can be drawn from the difficulties encountered to date?
- What will happen if these difficulties continue?

- Would a modified version of your product or service (streamlined or upgraded) have greater market appeal?
- What has to be changed/adapted from the previous approach?
- Does it make sense to order a "pause for thought" and develop new ideas?
- How could the invested time and financial resources potentially be deployed in a more rewarding way?
- If things continue unchanged, what is the likely result?

ANTI-CRASH FORMULA

Define clear turning points (firm halt lines) beforehand and obey them! Either abandon your project or adjust your goal by adapting it to the knowledge you have gained.

Of course, it is not fun, but visualizing the worst-case scenario before people start making the "close your eyes and hope for the best" argument can help you avoid disaster. The following item also concerns "worst cases."

Act Prudently: With the Caution of Edward A. Murphy

As an old American saying has it, "If it ain't broke, don't fix it." Although this cutely summarizes satisfaction with traditional ways of doing things, this maxim is not to be recommended. Once in a while things *do* need fixing, as catastrophes major and minor prove again and again. The more that is at stake, the more important it is to recognize when a project has gotten out of hand.

Murphy's Law as Guiding Principle

Worst-case scenarios are one way of making people aware of how events can differ from expectations. In the first chapter, we dealt with general scenarios for preparing for extreme situations, which might endanger a company as a whole. So it pays to counter this "planning fallacy" for individual projects by questioning your assumptions and considering what might go wrong. Take Murphy's Law—"Anything that can go wrong will go wrong"—seriously for once. What would this mean in specific, real-life scenarios? This consideration inevitably leads to certain questions. Let's consider a few.

Questions about Negative Developments

- What could go wrong?
- What are your key project assumptions?
- What happens if these assumptions *don't* fit?
- How do we recognize that they don't fit? What early indicators are there?
- Is it possible to test our assumptions (or have them tested by a third party) at a reasonable cost? Would it be possible (and helpful) to conduct market research, trial runs, and other forms of research?
- What would be the worst-case scenario? What would the early warning signs be?

Using the "Scenario Method"

By the way, this scenario technique pursues these questions comprehensively and extremely systematically. Potential developments are thoroughly analyzed in light of a variety of possible influences, and the results can be used to design and review business strategies. In doing so, positive as well as negative extreme scenarios are thought through to their logical conclusions.[69] Let's face it: the business world is never going to lack positive scenarios. In the end, this corresponds to the popular demand that managers face, namely, that they are supposed to fire up their employees and have them all enthusiastically cheering their "vision."

New: The Devil's Advocate on the Team

There is nothing wrong with that in principle. But is there anything to be said against choosing one of the more analytical, rational types on your team to be the devil's advocate, thus ensuring that an opposing point of view will always be heard? Warning voices have a bad reputation in some companies and are eagerly disparaged as a "drag" and "not team players." This attitude would be understandable if it was only targeted at unconstructive moaning and backbiting; however, if it targets those who seek to identify possible risks and ways to deal with them, it is harder to understand. It is also conceivable that for each "question" to be discussed in detail, a new devil's advocate be chosen. In the long run, this should ensure that critically thinking through counterarguments becomes a constructive habit.

---

69 Falko E. P. Wilms, ed., *Szenariotechnik. Vom Ungang mit der Zukunft* (Scenario Planning: How to Deal with the Future) (Bern: Haupt, 2006).

Possible Candidates for the Role of "Devil's Advocate"

Anyone who wishes to be an effective critic needs to distance himself from the project and look at it impartially. This bird's eye view is often easier for external observers than insiders, who prefer to see things with the department's view. Another option for risk control would be to bring in an impartial outsider, someone who ideally would be acceptable to everyone. It is often enough to have someone pose the right questions to uncover the weak points. Anything that cannot be explained convincingly probably has not been properly thought through. The critic's role can be filled by an external consultant, but also by an experienced mentor or a competent colleague— and sometimes even by the person who sits on the other side of the table at breakfast.

ANTI-CRASH FORMULA

Ensure that you maintain an overview of possible risks. For important projects, run through worst-case scenarios. Make sure that someone on your team assumes the role of "devil's advocate."

TARGET FIXATION—AND WHAT YOU CAN DO

Finally, here once again are all the measures you can put in place to avoid target fixation and associated carelessness.

ANTI-CRASH FORMULAS AT A GLANCE

1. The closer a goal appears to be, the more carelessness creeps in. Especially when the goal is in sight, keep a cool head.
2. It is more courageous to make a controlled emergency landing in hazardous situations than to risk a crash landing. Emergency landings are unpleasant, but less deadly than crashes.
3. Pay attention to your inner voice. Take warning if phrases like "It has to work," "It'll be all right," "There's no alternative," and "Close your eyes and hope for the best" start being bandied about. They are a signal that it is probably time to pull the emergency brake and take a calm, considered look at everything.

4. Keep in mind the old aviation saying: "There are old pilots; there are bold pilots, yet there aren't many old, bold pilots." The difference between courage and boldness is small but dangerous.

5. The best alarm system is useless when the warning signs are systematically ignored. Ensure that there are people surrounding you who take warning signs seriously. Establish a risk-control system.

6. The more enticing the goal is, the more (self-)critical you should be, because the greater the likelihood that you won't want to perceive the dangers. Ask yourself to what extent you are truly ready to give up your project and turn around. Be honest with yourself.

7. Regularly check your habits: What has been done differently recently and why? Which procedures have snuck in that, upon closer examination, harbor considerable risks?

8. Define clear turning points (firm halt lines) beforehand and obey them! Either abandon your project or adjust your goal by adapting it to the knowledge you have gained.

9. Ensure that you maintain an overview of possible risks. For important projects, run through worst-case scenarios. Make sure that someone on your team assumes the role of "devil's advocate."

CHAPTER 4

AIRPLANES GOING DOWN
AND NOBODY CARES

(Or What Happens When You Let Your Target Out of Sight)

+ + + December 29, 1972 + + + An Eastern Air Lines
Lockheed L-1011-1 Tristar crashes into the Florida
Everglades. + + + 101 dead + + +

"Hey, what's happening here?" The last words of
the captain of a Lockheed Tristar that crashed into
a swamp near Miami shortly after Christmas in 1972.
Three seconds later, the plane hit the surface of the
Everglades, killing the pilot and over 100 of the 163
people on board.[70]

How did this happen? An airplane's landing gear
is extended during its descent. Normally three green
lights should illuminate, one for each part of the

---

70 German Lockheed L1011 Information Center, www.eucomairlines.de/unfall/easte401.html.

undercarriage. But only two lit up. The plane's landing was aborted, and it started a holding pattern. At that point, the entire crew was focused exclusively on the little light that didn't illuminate: was it just that the light was broken, or had the forward landing gear really not extended? They lost sight of everything else. The captain, co-pilot, and the flight engineer were so focused on the problem that they didn't realize that the aircraft had started a leisurely descent. Only immediately prior to the crash did the crew realize that something was wrong. A broken warning light distracted them from all of the aircraft's other systems and controls—as well as from the fact that the autopilot had accidentally been switched off.

THE IMBALANCE BETWEEN ADMINISTRATION TIME AND TIME SPENT ADDING VALUE

"If you were to survey the CEOs of the 100 largest German companies about how much time they spend on administration, documentation, excessive micromanagement, dealing with plots, fixing mistakes and other problems caused by unnecessary complexity and how much time remains for future-oriented, value-improving and strategic tasks—then there is no doubt that much more time is spent on the first group than the second. I will set aside the question of whether the ratio is more like 70:30 or 99:1 in the individual cases."[71]

Is Risk Oversight a Foreign Word?

No, that wasn't written by a left-wing sociologist, but rather Utz Claasen, the former CEO of the German energy company EnBW. Claasen was a high flyer, who assumed control of one of Germany's largest energy suppliers at the age of forty and led the company for four and a half years. He is not the only person to have found it difficult to pick out the truly important from the huge tide of information during any business day. It's not just planes that crash whose crews don't notice it happening. There are also companies that reach the brink of

---

71 "Tendency towards Action," *Brand eins,* no. 3 (2008): 77.

bankruptcy without management even realizing. According to the survey quoted before, "79 percent of the insolvency administrators consider 'lack of oversight' to be a frequent cause of insolvency." And it gets even worse: "77 percent of the insolvency administrators had dealt with a company that had no costing and accounting."[72] There were probably also meetings held in these companies, new developments were discussed, product catalogues created, orders delivered, continuing professional development measures organized, and anniversaries celebrated. In other words, they were thoroughly occupied with everything going on in their business except for one vital question: Is all this effort actually making us enough money? Or have we been fiddling around with peripheral questions long after we started going into a descent?

CRASH EXAMPLE: MIAMI, DECEMBER 1972

Unbelievable Cause

An Eastern Air Lines plane that had only been in service for four months underwent a "controlled" crash on an internal flight from New York to Miami. That is, it crashed not due to mechanical failure or adverse weather conditions, but because the pilots misread the situation. This was the "first fatal accident involving a wide-body airliner"[73] and received massive public interest.

The Facts

Eastern Air Lines had had a perfect safety record to that date: no accidents had occurred since its founding seven years before, despite 1,400 flights daily.[74] The cause of the crash was unbelievably simple: one of the green warning lights, which indicated when the landing gear was extended, did not light up during landing. There are two possible causes for such warning light failures: either there really is a technical problem, or it's just the light that is broken. The latter is almost always the case, but of course, you need to probe the matter thoroughly. So the crew of Eastern Air Lines Flight 401 could not be sure if the nose landing gear had actually extended and was locked in place. After quickly consulting with air traffic control in Miami, the aircraft climbed back to 2,000 feet and began a holding pattern over

---

72   "Reasons for Bankruptcy," *Wirtschaft konkret,* no. 414: 7, 20.
73   German Lockheed L1011 Information Center, www.eucomairlines.de/unfall/easte401.html.
74   Waterkeyn, 106.

the Everglades swamps. While they circled at that height, the co-pilot activated the autopilot, according to the captain's instructions. The flight engineer climbed down into the electronics space underneath the cockpit, from where he was able to see whether or not the landing gear had actually extended. If the landing gear had failed to extend due to a problem with the hydraulics system, then the crew could have also extended the landing gear manually—so no particular cause for alarm.

The Procedures on Board

While the flight engineer was getting a bearing on the situation, the pilots were focused on the broken light bulb. According to the report issued by the Lockheed Information Center, they "unsuccessfully attempted to remove the nose gear light lens."[75] In addition to their conversations, the cockpit voice recorder documented a buzzing sound that the pilots apparently didn't notice. It was intended to notify the crew about deviation from the prescribed altitude. By the way, it was after 11:30 p.m. and pitch-black. While the pilots continued to debate about whether it would be better to remove the light bulb with a handkerchief, or even better a Kleenex, and whether a pair of pliers might be any help, the aircraft had long since left its course and was entering a slow but steady dive. At 23:40:38, crew overhear the altitude alarm's warning signal. At 23:41:40, the air traffic controller responsible noticed that the plane was flying very low. At this point in time, the plane was still at an altitude of 900 feet. The air traffic controller was tracking it on his radar screen. But all he said was "Eastern 401, how are things comin' along up there?" After the crash, he stated that he only initiated radio contact because the plane was approaching the airspace that he was responsible for. At the time, the air traffic controller was not required to issue information about altitude.[76] At 23:41:50, the pilots finally notice that something is not right: "Huh?" the captain said, and the co-pilot replied, "We did something to the altitude." The captain's answer: "What? We're still at 2000 [feet], right? . . . Hey, what's happening here?" The next moment, the airplane crashed into the Everglades, a swampy area with water up to the knees and teeming with alligators. One hundred and one of the 176 on board died.

75   German Lockheed L 1011 Information Center, ibid.
76   Ibid.

Real Cause of the Crash: Humans

The results of the subsequent investigation showed that one of the pilots presumably hit the control column and accidentally turned off the autopilot. This led to the descent. "Neither of the two pilots appeared to feel responsible for piloting the aircraft shortly before the crash. They were so involved with the nose landing gear indicator that they did not check the flight instruments during the last four minutes of flight," according to the German Lockheed L 1011 Information Center's report. The crash prompted the company to rework the warning lights and the autopilot elevation warning system. But in this case, too, the actual cause of the crash was not the equipment. Rather the responsibility for the accident lay with the crew, whose complete attention was drawn to one single detail and who forgot their true task: flying the plane safely at all times.

CRASH WARNING

First fly the aircraft! Do you still have your true task in view?

COMPANY EXAMPLE: DR. JÜRGEN SCHNEIDER— HOW TO PULL THE WOOL OVER BANKERS' EYES

A Real Estate Tycoon's Deals

Over 1,000 creditors, 2.4 billion DM in debts: this was the result of the Schneider bankruptcy in 1994. In the end, more than 100 pieces of real estate across Germany belonged to the tycoon's operation, including prestigious addresses like the Bernheimer Palais in Munich and the historic hotel Fürstenhof or the Mädlerpassage shopping arcade in Leipzig—not to mention 60 condominiums in Wiesbaden. Schneider's empire was financed by well-known banks, even when it became unavoidable to overlook that something wasn't quite right. For instance, with the construction of the Les Facettes shopping center in Frankfurt, Schneider led Deutsche Bank to believe there was a leasable surface area of 20,000 square meters (215,000 square feet) in a 2,000 square meter, eight-story property. According to my math, that makes 16,000 square meters—and that's only if the toilets and stairwells had also been leased for the astronomical asking price of 150

DM per square meter. Maybe one of the bankers should have taken a walk down to the construction site during his lunch break.

Schneider's Beautiful Illusion

Instead, the Schneider trial brought to light the "deeply amusing and disturbing." The *Frankfurter Allgemeine Zeitung* wrote in retrospect: "It became clear that the accused pulled the wool over the eyes of his business partners, all of them renowned and highly paid men of the German financial world, like a marriage swindler tricks well-heeled widows. In the cultivated ambiance of his company headquarters in noble Königstein, the Villa Andreae, he unfurled faked plans, impressed with pictures of shining house fronts and promised fantastical rates of return. Any child could have seen that Schneider's capital raising was based on fraud—only the bank directors were blind to it."[77]

Movie Material

Clearly, as a cunning self-publicist, Schneider understood how to draw the bankers' attention away from their basic task: to keep an eye on the numbers and scrutinize Schneider's business models closely, in order to avert poor investments and economic damage from their institutions. They let themselves be distracted by minor details and apparently basked in the society of the urbane financial juggler. It is all so outlandish that it was good enough for a good movie: *Peanuts—the Bank Pays for Everything*.[78] Neither pilots nor bankers are immune to completely losing sight of their real job.

Only the Results Count

It may have been examples like these that led Fredmund Malik, one of the most highly regarded consultants in Germany, to name "results orientation" the first and most important principle of effective leadership: "Management is the job whose purpose is achieving results or putting in the groundwork to make those results achievable." According to Malik, what really counts are not the efforts, labor, hours of work, glamorous appearances, public renown, or recognition. One might

---

77 Thomas Kirn and Jürgen Schneider, "Cheferotiker in einer Welt voller Baulust," *Frankfurter Allgemeine Zeitung*, June 28, 2007, www.faz.net.

78 The movie with Ulrich Mühe and Iris Berbin could be seen in theaters in 1996.

want to add, taking Schneider's example into consideration, "What counts is the output."[79] This requires a clear focus on the essentials, especially in economically difficult times. Sometimes, when the economy is good and demand is high, the business practically runs itself; this is the time when detours are least dangerous, when it is safe to devote time to secondary issues. At any other time, distraction can prove disastrous for the company.

First Diversionary Tactic: New Design

And yet, the sideshows are tempting, even and especially during difficult periods, when other questions should actually take top priority. The first thing the new board does for the faltering mid-sized laundry operation is to give it a new logo, a new advertising campaign, and an expensive product brochure. They hire a well-known agency and for months are so occupied with the new company image that hardly any time remains for the acute problem: Sales are too low. How can we win over new clients *now* and lower our costs to remain solvent? In the end, they have a chic new "corporate identity," but the company is unfortunately broke.

Second Diversionary Tactic: Fragmentation

An additional example: in a company that produces household appliances, no stones are left unturned in a debate about whether the on/off button on a new vacuum cleaner should be black or silver—a scene that for an outsider is hardly less disconcerting than the Kleenex debate in the crashing plane. This client had acquired a veritable hodgepodge of products over the previous few years to combat constantly sinking sales figures: from vacuums to grills, from heating appliances to stoves. What was missing was clear market positioning and a clear strategic orientation. Instead of recognizing that the current course of frantic and unthinking reaction was a one-way ticket to insolvency, they got lost in the details like the color of the vacuum cleaner switch. The sales force had long since despaired in the face of the company's illogical product portfolio, and the best workers had started packing their bags. The rest of the team was so busy integrating the constant acquisitions, standardizing the processes, and keeping the main business itself running that no one had the time or mental energy left that might have led them to question the

---

79   Fredmund Malik, *Managing Performing Living: Effective Management for a New Era* (Frankfurt: Campus Verlag, 2009), 73–74.

point of all this activity. All the while, the company kept on going downhill. You probably know how one could describe such situations: the lights are on, but no one's at home.

THE LIGHTS ARE ON, BUT NO ONE'S AT HOME

Directionless Reaction Instead of Planned Action

In the first chapter, we talked about the "reflex amoeba": fight, flight, play dead. When restless reaction is in control, the view for the essentials has long disappeared. Instead of planning prudently, people react ad hoc; instead of tackling the oncoming wall of flame, people extinguish only isolated sparks. In the worst case, this continues till the roaring fire rolls over everything. This comes as no surprise to the business psychologist Franz Reither. In an empirical study of behavior in complex situations, he was able to establish that, paradoxically, prudence and systematic planning retreat further and further into the background the more they are needed: "If the activity initially continues to be directed at actively shaping events, oriented at specific concepts and targets, this will often change as the problematic situation develops. The deeper one penetrates into the network of multi-faceted and also dynamic nexuses, the faster active, planned action transforms into a more or less passive reaction, reduced to attempting to tackle a series of new problems as quickly as they appear."[80] To put it plainly, the following principle carries the day: well, at least we are doing something!

Action at All Costs: At Least We Are Doing Something

Main Features of Actionism

People always speak of "actionism" when short-term, frequently hasty measures are taken that prove to be ineffective or even counterproductive in the medium term or long term. "Actionism" is the opposite of a well-thought-through, strategic approach, which is why people also speak of "blind" actionism. Of course, no one is ever an actor of "actionism" but just has (far) too much to do and "meets challenges proactively."

---

80 Reither, 58.

Actionism in All Areas of Life

Examples of "actionism" can be found everywhere: In private life, when people suddenly start cleaning windows with true devotion to the task or start tinkering in the garage instead of finally starting the unwelcome task of exam preparation. In politics, when billions are pumped into a short-term economic stimulus without any thought being given to the viability of the investment—such as "Cash for Clunkers" in 2009. This program did indeed delay the collapse in sales in the car market for a few months—at the taxpayers' expense—but given the massive overcapacity in the automobile industry, it obviously could do nothing to prevent it. In business, examples of "actionism" can always be found where frantic, superficial measures are taken in place of dealing with the root problem. For example, no more cookies in meetings to save money and the cleaners only come every second day—but otherwise it is business as usual. Or there is an immediate moratorium on business flights within Europe, overlooking the fact that an economy flight would not only be cheaper than the gas for Cologne to Barcelona and back, but would also tie up less productive work time. And before you dismiss this as a rant, consider that both examples are taken from real life.

What drives ad hoc decision making of this kind? You do not have to be a psychologist to guess why it is so tempting to flee into keeping busy when faced with a precarious situation.

Causes for (Blind) Actionism

- **Taking action is calming.** Having something to do gives us the illusion of being master of the situation, of having everything under control—or at least being in the process of getting it back under control. Most people find this less challenging than taking a moment to sit down and calmly reflect on the situation.
- **You immediately have results.** Ad hoc actions generally aim for immediate, short-term effects. The automobile industry was helped by the "Cash for Clunkers" program, but painful structural adjustments were only delayed.
- **You stay in familiar territory.** As a rule, spontaneous actions concentrate on fixing existing problems, not on fundamental, systemic changes. Change always means insecurity and, with that, always risk. For that reason, only very few people like real change; many prefer everything staying basically

the way it is. Anyone who has managed a transformation process can tell you about it. The final point is closely connected.

- **You don't have to admit that you have a fundamental (big) problem.** That is to say, you can avoid mentioning the problem for which comprehensive solution strategies have to be developed. And you can also forestall any accusation that you got things wrong in the past, by reacting too late to incipient dangers. Anyone who bans old-style light bulbs surely cannot be accused of not taking climate change seriously. Any anyone who goes so far as to ban managers from flying must really be determined to cut costs. Right?

Strategic Solutions? No Chance

The automobile industry offers additional examples regarding keeping busy. Instead of staring at the "Cash for Clunkers" program like the proverbial deer in the headlights, they should have laid the groundwork years before, as stated by Christian Homburg, president of the Mannheim Business School for Management. He senses a lack of "engagement with the long-term challenges" and "strategic vision on the part of management," and "not just in recent months." While Toyota, for example, recognized the sign of the economic times, Chrysler continued to produce gas guzzlers: "the managers reacted to the crisis with the usual reflexes: mandatory reduced hours, layoffs, factory closures . . . why were no strategic solutions offered?"[81] Activity in place of strategy, then, is essentially opening a box of Band-Aids instead of diagnosing the cause of the illness.

Which Type Are You?

But you do not have to go that far. Most of us probably recognize the phenomenon from our own lives. Say your child came home with a failing grade in math. Everything had been fine until now and suddenly this! Which of the following scenarios rings true? Scenario 1: You take a look at the F and start by leaning back calmly. You take time to analyze whether the grade is a slip-up or the beginning of a long-term trend. Together with your child, you develop a medium-term plan to bring the grades in math up to an average level by graduation. Or scenario 2:

---

81   "Managerversagen in der Autobranche: Die Weitsicht hat gefehlt" (Manager Failure in the Automobile Industry: The Foresight Was Lacking), *Manager Magazin*, April 6, 2009, www. manager.magazin.de.

You are very concerned and worry about what caused your child's sudden decline. You immediately start searching for a suitable math tutor. Of course, you will have conversations with the homeroom teacher and math teacher about what can be done. That same night, you order between two, three, four, or five math exercise books on the Internet. You try to understand the material yourself. In the end, you want to help your child. But maybe your child is not even bad at school; perhaps he just has ADHD? Of course, *you* would never react as extremely as in scenario 2, rushing headlong into frantic activity. But maybe you know someone that you could see going that far.

Escape into Details

Why do three men concentrate on one single warning light and completely lose sight of the overall situation? Why do automobile managers perfect the tiniest details on old models, instead of reconsidering their failing *business model*? Franz Reither writes, "The meticulous concentration on individual aspects, above all with those that one already knows well, transmits a justified feeling to others and oneself that one is competently and intensely engaging with the situation."[82] Such flight reactions are human, but that does not make them any better. Under pressure, we like to take refuge in what we know. We dive into "favorite tasks," overlook dangers, cling to a path once it has been chosen, and ignore all alternatives. Who likes to admit that he was wrong? Politicians want to be reelected, managers want to be promoted, and we all want to save face. The result is a rash reaction, instead of planned actions. It would be better to pause in the middle of all the bustle and pose a few key questions.

Key Questions
- Is what we are currently doing actually advancing our company?
- What is our most urgent problem currently?
- How much time are we devoting to this problem?
- How important is the problem we are currently focusing on?
- How much of what I am currently doing is contributing to solving our most urgent problem? Is it possible that I am focusing on my favorite task? Or am I trying to solve a new problem with an old (obsolete) solution?

---

82 Reither, 79.

ANTI-CRASH FORMULA

Pause for a moment and think: What, precisely, is the real problem? Is the current action solving the problem, or is it at least contributing to a solution? What would happen if you *didn't* start this action now?

The Difficulty of Seeing What Is Essential

The Disadvantages of Modern Communications

In most companies, it is becoming increasingly difficult for those who bear responsibility to keep the essentials in view. For many people, there is too much of everything in the normal workday: too many emails, too many phone calls, too many meetings, too many things "noted" as hedging, too much work in the first place. The easier communication has become technologically, the more that is being "communicated"—at least when viewed superficially. Anyone who had to type (or have typed) a letter was well advised to order his thoughts beforehand; otherwise, a time-consuming second draft threatened. In contrast, an email is quickly written and sent to dozens of people with a mouse click. This is (mis-)used to the full; the widespread "cc" mania has our inboxes overflowing. No one can read all of it, so as a result, no one even tries anymore. People muddle through one way or another. Many messages are only started or skimmed. With an email, you can assume that only the text in the reference line, which is visible, will be read. This leads to misunderstandings and generates yet more questions that have to be dealt with by email or on the phone.

Result: Brain Fade

The more specialization there is within a company, the more points of contact there are, then all the more time is spent by employees informing, agreeing, and double-checking with one another. The communication specialist Miriam Meckel derisively remarked years ago that the "flood of data" is inevitably followed by a "low tide of thought." But the low tide is more dangerous.[83] There

---

83 Miriam Meckel, *Das Glück der Unerreichberkeit* (The Fortune of Non-Availability) (Hamburg: Murmann Verlag, 2007).

is only one thing that there is definitely too little of: time to think through and set the right priorities.

The Eisenhower Principle

In the course of their respective careers (or CPD), almost everyone receives a supposedly simple tool designed to help identify what is truly important. I refer to the so-called "Eisenhower Principle," which the general and later US president used to sharpen his own awareness for the fundamentals. In this regard, he differentiated between "urgent" and "important." The difference is as follows: The dimension for "urgent" is time. The dimension for "important" is the goal. All activities that bring you closer to your goal are important. If your goal is acquiring new clients, then putting together your tax declaration is not an important activity, even if you expect a hefty tax refund. Neither important nor urgent things should be neglected and tossed into the trash can. Instead, Eisenhower recommended taking care of both urgent and important matters immediately. In addition, you should delegate (urgent, not important) and plan (important, not urgent). In all honesty, how often have you really applied these lessons at work? How often have you quickly taken care of urgent but unimportant pieces of work yourself, instead of delegating them? Most people clearly do not function as rationally as Mr. Eisenhower, either in the cockpit or at their desks.

The Tyranny of the Urgent

Most of the truly important things in life are not urgent. It basically does not matter if you begin to draft a new corporate strategy today or next month. If you put off to next week starting that fitness program your doctor recommended, it is not going to kill you—that is, if you start at all! The time management expert Lothar Seiwert characterizes this phenomenon of the truly important task being pushed aside by a multitude of urgent tasks as the tyranny of the urgent. He also coined a neat way to paraphrase the Eisenhower quadrants, which make the daily rush much easier to visualize than the sober division into A, B, and C tasks (see Fig. 2).

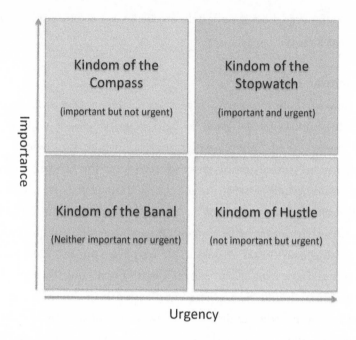

Figure 2: Focusing on the essentials, from Seiwert's *The Boomerang Principle.*[84]

"Urgent" Tasks Distract

If you go through your daily schedule, you might find, to your dismay, that you spend most of your time in the "kingdom of the banal" or the "kingdom of hustle." People are positively consumed by details that cry out for their attention, while postponing the truly important tasks from week to week or month to month—if not year to year. Much of what people do out of good nature or habit, or also as a reflex reaction to particularly strong signals (the ringing telephone, the "urgent" employee question), barely contributes to the company's core business. That is why I speak of "intrusive" issues; that description appears more fitting than the neutral "urgent."

The Kingdom of the Compass as Goal

The more frequently you spend time in the "kingdom of hustle" or the "kingdom of the banal," the greater the danger that you will be forced into the "kingdom

---

84 Lothar Seiwert, *Das Bumerang-Prinzip: Mehr Zeit fürs Glück* (The Boomerang Principle: More Time for Happiness), 2nd ed. (Munich: DTV, 2005), 120.

of the stopwatch" and have to apply rapid damage control. For example, the appointment with the auditor or the bank is prepared badly at the last minute; the key client who is complaining is called back much too late; decisions about the reorientation of the product range are made under high pressure. The "kingdom of the compass" is now only a distant dream. Yet that is the place to make the strategic decisions that are important for the survival and growth of the company. Anyone who never or only infrequently makes it there runs the risk of one day being shocked like the Lockheed pilot, recognizing the seriousness of the situation just before the crash, with a belated "Hey, what's going on?" This can only be prevented by brute force, as it were; you must systematically keep some time free for thought. Whether that is an hour every week, one morning every month, or a day every quarter depends on your work habits. Block off these times in your calendar, and treat them as seriously as any other appointment. What should you be doing during these appointments? Here, as well, there is a nice image from aviation: "staying ahead of the aircraft." Make sure that you're always a step ahead of the current situation.

ANTI-CRASH FORMULA

Make sure urgent matters don't prevent you from recognizing the truly important things—and tackle them concretely! Systematically and consistently block off "thinking and strategy time."

SITUATIONAL AWARENESS: STAYING AHEAD OF THE AIRCRAFT

Thinking Ahead

Judicious planning that keeps a company safely on track and also avoids reactive panic in difficult times: that is the goal. And that is also the focus in every cockpit. Every experienced flight instructor passes the formula for success of "staying ahead of the aircraft" on to his students. Whoever wants to be in control of the situation at all times has to know where he is at a given moment and what the next important steps are. To put it another way, "Never let an airplane take you somewhere your brain didn't get to five minutes earlier," as pilots are rightfully fond of saying.

Awareness for the Current Situation: Where Do We Stand?

Striving for Situational Awareness

A pilot who wants to get his aircraft to the target airport safely should be completely aware of the current situation in the aircraft at all times. "Situational awareness" denotes this consciousness and alert analysis of current events at every point in time during the flight. Just *assuming* that everything is progressing normally is dangerous, as Lockheed Flight 401 shows. If the crew had only taken one look at the instruments right in front of their noses, then they would not have remained oblivious to the fact that their plane had long departed from its prescribed course and, above all, the prescribed elevation. Of course, situational awareness is not just about altitude and courses, but also about flawlessly functioning technology, sufficient fuel, conditions at the target airport, the situation in the air, and the weather conditions—so just about everything that influences the flight now and in the future.

In the business context, situational awareness is achieved by asking pertinent questions:

- Where do we stand?
- Are all processes currently working flawlessly?
- Do we have sufficient cash reserves ("fuel")?
- Are the key performance indicators in the black?
- What is happening around us ("airspace")?
- What is the situation like in our market segment? ("Is someone getting too close?")
- What is the economic forecast? ("Do storms and severe weather threaten?")
- What are the economic prospects for our most important clients?

Chain Reaction Bound to Occur

Only those who can reliably say where they stand really have the situation under control. And only those who evaluate the situation with some certainty can make the right decisions—decisions about what should happen at a given time and what the next relevant steps are. Whoever loses this oversight will waver and hesitate when he has to make a decision. And you do have to expect nasty surprises. In turn, nasty surprises mean stress, and in many cases, stress means tunnel vision and aimlessness (short-term, ad hoc action instead of effective measures). This is true for aviation as well as on the ground. As a pilot, I can't stand surprises!

The Problem: Insufficient Oversight

Today, every airplane is packed with systems and instruments that facilitate the pilot's exact analysis of the current situation. Today, such instruments are also available to professionally led companies in the form of operating numbers, sales lists, and turnover data. Modern auditing now supplies an abundance of analyses from all possible viewpoints. In both cases, the problem is less a lack of data and information and more a lack of oversight. Which data is actually important? In some companies, a never-ending flood of Excel spreadsheets overflows on the desks, but hardly anyone is able to adequately comprehend or even analyze the deluge of numbers. Instead, managers delude themselves into thinking they are safe because everything is precisely calculated—surely meaning the situation is under control and everything is ok. There it is again: the illusion of control. That is why there are companies whose sales continuously increase and, at the same time, continue to register increasingly high losses.

Figure 3: Situational awareness in business (key factors).

For instance, consider the product range of the manufacturer of household appliances mentioned before that was out of control. You can grow to death. Although other companies recognize that their profits are decreasing from year to year, those in positions of responsibility still repeatedly manage to find "proof" in the mountains of data that the company is about to turn the corner. If you look hard enough, you are sure to be able to interpret the data the way you want. That wishful, delusional line of thinking is why it is best to immunize yourself to this danger through mindful concentration on the key factors that form the basis for situational awareness.

Fact-Check Regularly

Situational awareness means having the important facts in view for each of these areas:

- Who are our most important clients? What is the client structure like? Is there a dangerous dependence on a few key clients?
- Who are the central competitors? What kind of dynamics do the competitors unleash? How large is their market share? How well are we prepared for the future in comparison to them? What separates our offer from that of the competition?
- Is our product range up to date? With which products do we achieve the majority of our profits? Are we recording stable or decreasing sales? Are our most important sources of revenue (cash cows) still working?
- Do we have sufficient liquidity? What is our clients' payment behavior? Do we have to expect defaults in payments? How is our creditworthiness rated? Can we expect our banks to support us?
- Do we have a clearly formulated strategy? In which direction should the company develop?
- What are the legal and societal conditions? How will our company be judged in the court of public opinion? Do we know and fulfill all the legal requirements?
- Do we know the market precisely? Have we exhausted all its potential?
- Does purchasing work seamlessly (suppliers, raw materials)?

Paul A. Craig, veteran American pilot and multiple award-winning flight instructor, demands a "mental radar screen" from accomplished pilots, a continually updated overview of their own situation and surroundings[85]—a characteristic that successful entrepreneurs no doubt share.

ANTI-CRASH FORMULA

Do you know at all times where your company (your department) stands? Do you have all the relevant facts and data from the business environment in view?

Thinking Ahead: What Could Happen? What Are the Next Steps?

Using the Quiet Phases

It was jokingly claimed the pilot's brain should always be thinking five minutes ahead. You probably heard of "planning ahead" in your car driving lessons, and, in fact, it is not highly recommended to think of applying the brakes only when you are two meters from a red light. An alert car driver registers children playing next to the roadway before they jump into the street, and the driver anticipates that the bus further back will soon turn and merge with traffic again. The same applies to flying: good pilots use calm phases to prepare as much as possible. When they roll onto the tarmac, the start and takeoff has already been prepared. All navigational instruments and systems are set for takeoff. During cruising, the approach and landing are being prepared. Corresponding maps are made ready for alternate routes, too. All radio frequencies are set, and the landing process is talked through. Everything that can be taken care of or prepared during the quiet periods can then simply be called up "at the touch of a button." If something unexpected happens, the pilots have all their resources available to work towards a solution for the problem. If perfectly normal, everyday business in a company is so preoccupying that you do not have any mental capacity available for thinking ahead, then it is high time to reconsider the distribution of responsibilities, procedures, and processes.

---

85   Paul A. Craig, *Pilot in Command: A Strategic Action Plan for Reducing Pilot Error* (New York: MacGraw-Hill, 1999), 48.

ANTI-CRASH FORMULA

Think: Are you always at least one step ahead of the current situation? Or is your attention completely absorbed by current events and details?

What Would Happen If . . .

An experienced pilot will never give in to the temptation to "switch off" during the quiet phases of a flight. Alertness is also required when everything seems to be going "normally"—just to be sure that it is actually the case (and that the autopilot has not gone offline unnoticed). Previously I wrote that flying is 99 percent routine and 1 percent pure panic. Whoever keeps everything in mind during the routine procedures and plans ahead for the worst case is best placed to avoid the life-threatening panic reaction. In his "Strategic Action Plan," Paul A. Craig advises pilots to systematically go through possible difficulties, like the weather changing, emergency landing, and so on, during the "boring" phases of the flight, under the category "What if?" What would you do if you suddenly ran out of fuel? What if you lost visual contact with the landing strip during the approach? Furthermore, Craig challenges pilots to think about the future like a top tennis player, mentally anticipating the game: "You have to have a plan, a strategy. You are thinking two and three shots ahead."[86] This way, rude surprises that require an ad hoc reaction become the exception.

Negative Example: Quelle

This form of anticipation is needed in businesses. It is tempting to lean back during the good times because everything apparently "takes care of itself." Where that leads can be observed from the example of the mail-order company Quelle, which also reacted too late to changing consumer habits, missed out on online sales (in contrast to its competitor Otto), and then finally had to be liquidated after a frantic bailout during the run-up to the German national elections in 2009. Winter catalogues could still be printed thanks to a state-financed loan to the tune of €50 million (which was backed by the Bavarian minister-president Horst Seehofer), but up till the very end, no viable business plan saw the light of day. "Something must be done" says hello again.

---

86   Ibid., 41.

ANTI-CRASH FORMULA

Do you take specific precautions against nasty surprises? Or do you take comfort in the illusion that everything will always remain the same? If the latter is the case, then you have to change your position.

So "staying ahead of the aircraft" first and foremost means to systematically think ahead about what could come, and second, actively plan ahead for the next steps in every situation. Keep in mind these relevant questions for a business context:

- Could it be the case that our key technology will soon be made obsolete by new developments?
- Are competitors explicitly trying to poach the market segments we are aiming for? How vulnerable are we to attacks from innovative start-ups?
- Do we use all the relevant sales channels? Or are we lagging behind on new possibilities; for instance, those offered by the Internet (blogs, Twitter, social media marketing)? Do the new possibilities fit with us and our products?
- Are some changes in customer expectations in sight that we have to react to in time? What does this mean for our range of products, for our marketing?
- Have the benefits that we offer our customers been increasing over the past 24 months or slowly fading?
- Are cash-flow problems caused by a high number of payments not received a possibility? Have we planned ahead for any sales slumps? Are there any medium-term, high-cost investments (production plants, buildings, personnel)?
- Are there any environmental regulations or pieces of new legislation that could force us to change course? Do we have "skeletons in the closet" that we would be well advised to bury properly?
- Could important foreign markets disappear due to political developments? Or, on the contrary, are new markets opening up?

- Would we be adequately prepared for a crash of our IT servers? Are there other technical areas where collapse would endanger the company's existence?

- Could prices for raw materials or upstream products rise drastically? Are our suppliers really the most suitable in the medium term (reliability, cost optimization)?

- Are we equipped for a generational change? Has the question of succession been cleared up?

- Are we doing things in a certain way just because we have "always done it that way"? Are there better alternatives?

Positive Company Example

A mid-sized consulting firm from my circle of clients, specializing in logistics software, had become the market leader through such prescient action. This company is actually always "ahead of the aircraft." Above all, this means not resting on your laurels, but instead already developing the next software "cash cow" before the current successful model has served its purpose. This is how a range of products was developed, from logistics software to a digital logbook that loosened the dependence of the company on individual large clients. A company that acts proactively in a similar way is Google. Instead of putting up their feet in light of booming profits, the company continues to offer new services—from Google Earth to the controversial digitalization of entire libraries.

ANTI-CRASH FORMULA

Do you still call the shots? Do you act confidently in the marketplace? Very good. Or do you only react to external influences? Then there is a need to act.

So the goal consists in systematically planning the future of a company. This can only work when the daily business is so well organized that it does not absorb 100 percent of your attention and people are not constantly firefighting somewhere. Good management is the be-all and end-all—there are numerous books about this. To finish, we will concentrate on a fundamental problem of modern organizations: their increasing complexity.

PROFESSIONAL BUSINESS MANAGEMENT

Prescriptions against Hasty or Tardy Decisions

Hustle and bustle is in charge at many companies today. Most managers and technical workers complain about a chronic lack of time. The result: many decisions are made hastily. Or, on the contrary, they are kicked into the long grass. The more connected the world economy is, the more differentiated the work at an organization is, the more ambitious a project is, then the more difficult it is for individuals to keep an overview of things and make the truly necessary happen. It would be foolhardy to promise a catch-all solution. Instead, what follows are several suggestions.

Avoiding Project Cascades and Debate Culture

Signals Take Time

A business responds—just like an aircraft—with a certain delay. If you use an aircraft's controls—for example, using the yoke to activate the elevators—it takes a few seconds for the plane to respond. For someone unfamiliar with this situation, those few seconds can feel like an eternity. Because the system does not react instantly, the individual is tempted to send new or stronger signals. But, of course, the system does react—just not straightaway. Unfortunately, by then, the new signal has already been transmitted, and the signals that have previously been sent catch up with you. The aircraft shakes and shudders. You will have seen the same effect in business. Any business (and, at the end of the day, the economy as a whole) is a delayed reaction system. The system reacts, but not instantly. Thanks to our hunger for quick, visible results, we frequently act impulsively and, indeed, overreact.

Causes of Project Cascades

You will certainly have experienced this manic tinkering yourself. Upper management announces a new strategic direction, initiating a whole series of projects in the individual departments. Before these projects have any chance of bearing fruit, the controls are taken in hand once again and a new course set. The new course means a plenitude of new measures to be taken, at every level of the business. The next wave of projects roll through the business before the previous one has ebbed and revealed its results. Some companies repeat this pattern and find themselves in a state of permanent reorganization, with no one able to tell which measures have led to which results anymore.

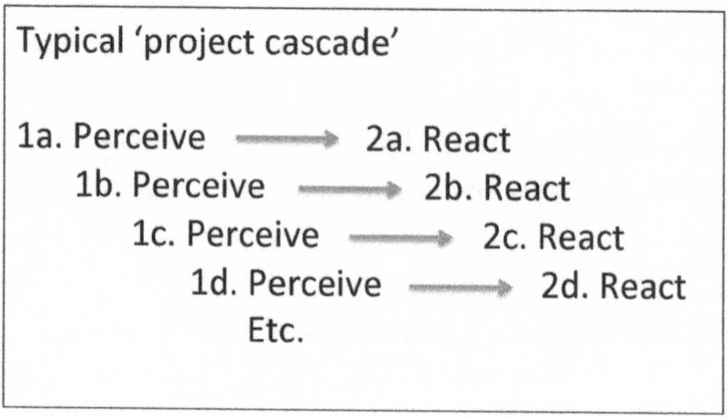

Typical 'project cascade'

1a. Perceive ⟶ 2a. React
   1b. Perceive ⟶ 2b. React
      1c. Perceive ⟶ 2c. React
         1d. Perceive ⟶ 2d. React
         Etc.

Figure 4: Typical project cascade.

The Chairmen: An Ejector Seat?

The increasingly short durations of chairpersons contribute to such cascades. The strategy consultancy Booz & Company examined the change in management in 2,500 largest publically traded companies under the headline "CEO Succession" and observed that the chairs belonging to top managers are increasingly becoming ejections seats. Managers in Europe are under even more pressure than their colleagues in the United States: "Underperformance leads top German managers to fail twice as frequently as their US colleagues . . . in Europe, a CEO is forced out after two or three years." The experts also gave the following warning in 2005: "CEOs that are forced out after two to three years due to underperformance have far too little time to show sustainable results."[87]

---

87   The innovations report from May 19, 2005, www.innovations-report.de/html/berichte/ studien/bericht-44490.html. In the meantime this insight appears to have reached some advisory boards; despite the financial crisis the consultancy registered slightly decreased fluctuation in top management positions in 2008. In Germany 17 percent of the CEOs had moved on during that time, 2,7 percent less than in 2007. (Press release Booz & Company from May 12, 2009, www.presseportal.de/meldung/1403382).

Impact on Employees

Everything is supposed to be better with a new boss. Yet every newcomer wants first to put down a marker and initiate changes, making it clear to everyone at the company that a new era has begun. A zoologist might say he's marking his territory. It is an open secret that far from all measures enacted in this context are sensible. Things will be done differently, but not necessarily better. Only in the medium term will it be possible to determine whether the measures really are an improvement and reduce costs, increase sales, or make the company better equipped to handle the future. And by the time that medium term has been reached, it is possible that another course has already been embarked upon. This puts companies in a state of permanent reorientation—and some employees in a state of stoic indifference. "We'll outlast this one too," is the reaction. Or employees may say, "Bosses come and go, but everything here stays the same." A good part of the complexity that affects daily business is self-generated, rather than being due to inevitable, extrinsic demands.

How Piloting Should Work

In business, just as in the cockpit, piloting should consist of a cycle with five steps (see Fig. 5).

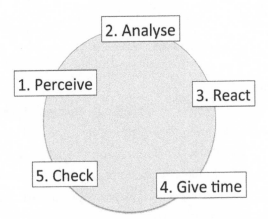

Figure 5: Piloting cycle in business.

Particularly in critical situations, it is almost impossibly difficult to wait after using the controls and give the system a chance to react to the signal.

Doing anything else, however, results in individual attempts to maneuver canceling each other out or even initiates a mutually amplified vicious cycle. Oddly enough, it is a rarity that frantic, panicky uses of the controls produce a virtuous circle of effects.

ANTI-CRASH FORMULA

The grass doesn't grow faster if you pull at it. A stimulus needs time to develop its effect, so shift down a gear.

Too Much Chatter . . .

But real life, in difficult economic (or airborne) situations, is dominated either by "doing something" with the typical project cascades or by the other extreme, namely, an unwillingness to do anything, instead engaging in discussion without results.

Debate culture - lethargy and fear of decision-making

1. Perceive ⟶ 2. Analyze, debate, more analysis, even more debate ⟶ END

Figure 6: Debate culture.

. . . Creates Lethargy

Many companies are quick to spot a threatening situation. They are also quick to start with the analysis. However, they don't get any further. They talk and discuss, discuss and talk. All the while, the company drifts further into crisis, rudderless, with no one at the helm. Just like aircraft, companies need someone at the controls; they need leadership. Sinking into lethargy is as fatal as rash overreaction. Of course, all the talk provides a fig leaf of activity.

Negative Example from Experience

The consequences are particularly tragic for individuals, for the employees—regardless of whether their place in the hierarchy is high or low. A mid-sized automobile parts supplier that I worked with some time ago is a fitting example. Based in southern Germany, it had 500 employees. It had been long clear that things were only getting worse for the industry. Worse, thanks to failure to audit the work of a key account manager (of the "not to be trusted with responsibility" type), a whole series of loss-making orders were in the books. Each order was tantamount to shipping money to the customer along with the parts delivered. An independent consultant was called in, and his findings finally made it impossible to ignore the terrible state the company found itself in. But instead of acting vigorously, one meeting after another was called. The main content of these gatherings was the question "Who's to blame for the dilemma?" It might not have been too late, but measures were briefly considered with hardly anything being done in practice. Along with the question of blame, the very next meeting would revolve around the "failure" of the measures decided in the last one. Six months ago, I learned that this company is now bankrupt. More than 500 people lost their livelihoods.

Your chances of survival in an airplane are significantly higher if you make a *bad* decision rather than making *no* decision. A bad decision has bad effects. But if you have your wits about you, you recognize these effects and can counteract them. In other words, you can correct the bad decision with a good decision. A decision not made (a non-decision) also has effects. These effects are just as fatal as the bad option. But these effects are usually not regarded as the result of decisions not made, but rather as the result of "circumstances" (like the "economic situation" or the "financial crisis"). The plane speeds towards a mountain, yet no one was "responsible." After all, no one *did* anything. The mountain was at fault! It makes much more sense to actively intervene in the system. At least you will learn something.

ANTI-CRASH FORMULA

No decision is also a decision. Hesitating to make a decision is devastating in a similar way to keeping busy for the sake of being busy. Guard yourself against passivity.

"Systematic Waste Disposal" (Malik)

What Makes Companies Sluggish

"Companies . . . aren't founded in order to establish a particularly modern way of accounting, a highly developed personnel department, a computer-supported administration or brilliant staff work. They are founded to create satisfied customers, develop and produce and sell products or services," emphasized the management guru Fredmund Malik at the end of his book *Managing Performing Living*.[88] The ironic references above point to the way in which the means within a company become the ends themselves. Together, they create a sluggish, bureaucratic monolith, with the system bloated and the really important questions obscured from view. Take time out to think through questions that will help you examine your situation critically.

Critically Examine Processes

- What is done in your company only because "it's always been done that way"?
- Which meetings regularly take place, even though most participants are more occupied with their smartphones than the contents of the meeting?
- Which meetings were called at short intervals, even though it would be sufficient to meet less frequently, possibly also in a smaller group?
- Which lists or statistics are recorded meticulously only to go unread and disappear into a file?
- Which clients are you carrying—the ones who contribute little in the way of profit and much in the way of effort and trouble?
- Which products and services continue to be offered despite (after being soberly assessed) no longer being profitable (or no longer matching the core business)?
- Which divisions of roles and responsibilities preserve and force Byzantine internal communications on the company, while offering little in the way of value?
- Which internal programs or measures (for instance, in the area of continuous professional development or internal communications) were

---

88 Malik, 326.

at some point started and never stopped, although their usefulness can be called into question?

Emergency Aid: Systematic Waste Disposal (Cleaning Up Is Called For)

The list could go on infinitely. Like all complex systems, companies also occasionally develop a life of their own, which can come as something of a shock for outsiders. Much that is complicated or extravagant (much that exists at all, in fact) thanks its existence to nothing more than the vagaries of historical development or homemade complexity, so to speak. Fredmund Malik has a simple and radical method to tackle this problem: "systematic waste disposal." The renowned management consultant recommends regularly posing this question, to your team, your department, or to management: "What, of what we do today, would we not start from the beginning if we weren't already doing it?"[89]

Take Out the Trash

Malik's question might not be the most elegant linguistically, but it is pure genius methodologically. The question forces us to make a sober assessment of the present and motivates us to act. However, in everyday business the question more commonly asked is "Why in the world did we do that?" This form of the question usually just introduces a rant—without results. Instead, Malik's question steers our attention to the current possibilities for change. Clean up your company and your department regularly! Once a year, think about which ballast you should throw overboard. And why not reserve an extra day, together with your team, to hunt out senseless, time-consuming, and outdated tasks and processes? There is worth in clearing the air for a better overview and ability to concentrate on the essentials.

ANTI-CRASH FORMULA

Operate a system of "waste disposal." Regularly examine what you do and eliminate the sideshows.

---

89 Ibid., 324.

OPERATIVE RUSH—AND WHAT YOU CAN DO

In conclusion, here are all the measures with which you can avoid getting lost in the details.

ANTI-CRASH FORMULAS AT A GLANCE

1. Pause for a moment and think: What, precisely, is the real problem? Is the current action solving the problem, or is it at least contributing to a solution? What would happen if you *didn't* start this action now?

2. Make sure urgent matters don't prevent you from recognizing the truly important things—and tackle them concretely! Systematically and consistently block off "thinking and strategy time."

3. Do you know at all times where your company (your department) stands? Do you have all the relevant facts and data from the business environment in view?

4. Think: Are you always at least one step ahead of the current situation? Or is your attention completely absorbed by current events and details?

5. Do you take specific precautions against nasty surprises? Or do you take comfort in the illusion that everything will always remain the same? If the latter is the case, then you have to change your position.

6. Do you still call the shots? Do you act confidently in the marketplace? Very good. Or do you only react to external influences? Then there is a need to act.

7. The grass doesn't grow faster if you pull at it. A stimulus needs time to develop its effect, so shift down a gear.

8. No decision is also a decision. Hesitating to make a decision is devastating in a similar way to keeping busy for the sake of being busy. Guard yourself against passivity.

9. Operate a system of "waste disposal." Regularly examine what you do and eliminate the sideshows.

CHAPTER 5

"BUT I THOUGHT *YOU* WERE FLYING!"

(Or When Responsibilities Are Blurred)

- -

+ + + 1990s + + + Kai Tak approach + + + "Pilotless" airliner comes into land—hard. + + + Passengers have their teeth rattled. + + +

In the cockpit, roles are very clearly defined. One pilot flies; the other ensures that everything else runs smoothly. It is just that it does not always work that way in practice. In the cockpit of a Boeing 747, the tension had been building for a while. The co-pilot is the pilot flying, but that hasn't stopped the captain from repeatedly interfering, which certainly is not improving the atmosphere. As they touch down at Kai Tak, a less than perfect approach is crowned by an extremely hard landing. After the two pilots have talked things over and cleared the air during the obligatory debriefing, the captain says, "Come on. Admit it; that was the worst landing you've ever flown." The co-pilot's responded, "Me? *You* were the one flying!" The captain had meddled in what the co-pilot was doing so often that it was no longer clear who was doing what. The roles were no longer clearly defined.

KAI TAK: HONG KONG'S "FEARED AIRPORT"

This anecdote is familiar to almost every pilot, a cautionary tale oft cited in training. Landing at the old Hong Kong International, Kai Tak, was always a tricky proposition. Mountains barred the approach to the solitary runway so that airliners were forced to bank right shortly before landing, skimming the rooftops of Kowloon. In addition, the tarmac (on reclaimed land in the harbor) was surrounded by the water on three sides. The idea that a passenger airliner touched down here with effectively no one at the controls is certainly a chilling one. Kai Tak was finally replaced by the more favorably situated Chek Lap Kok Airport in 1998.

WORKING IN A BAD ATMOSPHERE

There could hardly be a better way to illustrate the dangers of ill-defined responsibilities than with this aviation anecdote. For aircraft to fly safely and businesses to be run without incident, everyone must do his job reliably. If that isn't the case, then with some luck, everything might just carry on as normal. If that luck runs out—if the economy is faced with recession, or something unexpected happens in the air—then things can start going wrong, fast. Core tasks being neglected because of a "bad atmosphere" is a worryingly frequent occurrence.

CRASH EXAMPLE: MINNEAPOLIS, OCTOBER 2009

Missing the Airport

Have you ever missed an exit on the freeway because you were caught up in a heated discussion with the person in the passenger seat? Unfortunately, this can happen just as easily in the air as on the road. In October 2009, one such story made headlines that would have left any commercial flyers that day sweating. *Süddeutsche Zeitung*: "150 Miles Too Far." *Kölner Stadt-Anzeiger*: "Pilots Miss Airport."[90]

A Northwest Airlines flight from San Diego to Minneapolis overflew its destination airport. Only when a stewardess asked when they were finally going to land did the pilots realize their mistake and turn back. In the meantime, fighter jets were being put on alert, as it was feared that the plane had been hijacked. The Airbus 320, with 149 people on board, had lost contact with air traffic control at 19:00, and it was only reestablished at 20:14.

Chatting, Not Flying

The pilots, two old hands with many thousands of hours of flight time between them, told the Federal Aviation Administration (FAA) that they were distracted by "dealing with some company issues" (an intense discussion of a computerized rota system), causing them to lose track of their position. Speculation that the crew might have fallen asleep was rejected. The FAA condemned the behavior in the cockpit as careless and reckless. In light of the fact that, despite being directly responsible for scores of human lives, the two pilots clearly preferred to have a chat rather than do their job, the judgment sounds mild. Within days, both had their licenses revoked.[91]

A Clear Division of Responsibilities at Work?

You may shake your head at the thought of such negligence, but can you say with 100 percent certainty that in *your* business, your department, or your team, everyone is focusing entirely on what he is paid to do? Or do you sometimes get the uneasy feeling that internal squabbles, a lack of coordination, and unclear boundaries are consuming more energy than the actual job itself, putting the success of the business in danger? Companies—large and small—are by no means immune to this problem.

---

90 *Süddeutsche Zeitung*, October 23, 2009, www.sueddeutsche.de; *Kölner Stadt-Anzeiger*, October 24, 2009, www.ksta.de.

91 "240 Kilometer verflogen. Irrflug-Piloten verlieren Lizenz" (Lost their way by 240 Kilometers: Odyssey Pilots Lose Their License), *Süddeutsche Zeitung*, October 23, 2009, www.sueddeutsche.de.

CRASH WARNING

If responsibilities in key areas are unclear or are lost sight of due to internal disputes, a crash might be imminent.

COMPANY EXAMPLE: AIRBUS—
TWO MASTERS LEAD TO LEADERSHIP CRISIS

The Conundrum of the Chicken and the Egg: Which Came First?

"Airbus problems spark leadership crisis," announced German business magazine *Wirtschaftswoche* in June 2006.[92] Persistent delays in the delivery of the new A380 superjumbo had led to the share price falling by up to a third and put senior management at parent company EADS under massive pressure. Anyone following the press coverage of the company's woes in those weeks might have begun to ask himself whether, in truth, the real situation might be the other way round. Were problems at the executive level one of the main factors to blame for the massive delays to the flagship A380?

Dual Leadership Structure at EADS

At this point in time, aerospace and armaments giant EADS permitted itself an unusual management set up, with *two* CEOs (one French, one German) and *two* chairmen (again, one French, one German). The motivation behind this was the company's complex ownership structure. EADS had been created by the merger of a number European aerospace and defense contractors. At the time of the crisis, the French and Germans each had a 22.5 percent stake in the business. Spanish government held 5.5 percent of shares, and the remainder were held by private individuals and British investors.[93] To balance out this complex power structure, a dual leadership system was decided upon, with the Frenchman Noël Forgeard and the German Tom Enders being made CEOs. It might be worth pointing out here that until his promotion in June 2005, Forgeard had been head of Airbus and had expected to take over sole leadership

---

92 "Airbus Problems Spark Leadership Crises," *Wirtschaftswoche*, June 15, 2006, www.wiwo.de.
93 "Führungsstreit bei EADS beendet" (Leadership Quarrel at EADS Is Over), *Handelsblatt*, July 2, 2006, www.handelsblatt.com.

of EADS—an ambition that he had failed to push through.[94] It doesn't exactly sound like the beginning of a beautiful friendship, running a corporation turning over around $50 billion annually.

Tensions in the Parent Company

When delivery dates for the spectacular double-deck airliner had to be pushed back for the second time, Forgeard professed his surprise at the problems (claiming only to have been made aware of the difficulties in April)[95] and stated publicly, "When I was head of Airbus, we never missed our own projections."[96] This was a pointed attack on the German Airbus chief, Gustav Humbert. Although disastrous news was becoming a regular occurrence and major customers were threatening to cancel their orders, damage limitation seemed to be far from the executives' primary concern. In addition, Forgeard was in the sights of the French financial authorities under suspicion of insider trading, having made a multi-million-euro profit selling EADS shares in March.

Carrying the Can

On June 26, even Forgeard's patron, President Jacques Chirac, was moved to publicly call the dual leadership model into question in a television broadcast. Less than a week later, the game was up; both Forgeard and Airbus boss Humbert were forced out. However, the dual management structure was left in place, although the principal German shareholder, DaimlerChrysler, was also said to be unhappy with it. At least, though, as the *Frankfurter Allgemeine Zeitung* reported: "The operational responsibilities of the two EADS co-CEOs have been reshuffled, strengthening Tom Enders's position and leaving him in charge of the aviation business."[97] One might even conclude that the previous division of responsibilities had been less than optimal.

---

94 "Machtkampf und Krise bei EADS" (Power Struggle and Crisis at EADS), *Manager Magazin*, July 2, 2006, www.manager-magazin.de.
95 Ibid.
96 "Airbus-Probleme lösen Führungskrise aus" (Airbus Problems Spark Leadership Crises), *Wirtschaftswoche*, June 15, 2006; www.wiwo.de.
97 "Top Manager der EADS treten zurück" (Top Manager of EADS Quits), *Frankfurter Allgemeine Zeitung*, July 3, 2006, www.fazfinance.net.

Further Complications

But the story of EADS, Airbus, and the A380 prestige project doesn't end there. Addendum 1: One year later, EADS did finally do away with the dual leadership model. Forgeard's successor Louis Gallois became sole CEO with a German chairman at his side, and former co-CEO Tom Enders was made head of EADS's most important subsidiary, Airbus.[98] Addendum 2: On December 30th 2008, Airbus boss Enders toasted the delivery of the first dozen aircraft with champagne. However, as the *Neue Zürcher Zeitung* reported: "The first 25 aircraft need to be rewired by hand, since a different software version was used in the Hamburg factory than at the Toulouse, France, site, and parts didn't fit together."[99]

Effect on Employee Morale

Effective collaboration demands a genuine willingness to cooperate. Many "alpha types" have some difficulty with this, and examples can be found not just in multinational corporations, but in family businesses too. At one of my clients, two sales managers (one responsible for Germany, the other for the international key-account business) had concentrated their efforts on fighting a running battle for supremacy with each other. Eventually, this led to their teams spending more time on mutual recrimination and verbal nitpicking—such as who knew what, when—than they did doing their actual jobs and winning business for the company. Once conflict of this nature becomes engrained, EADS's radical solution of firing one of the warring parties may indeed be the best way out.

Turf Wars

Oddly, the business world still seems to believe that a successful organization can be created by throwing complete strangers together, who will then get down to it and somehow manage to find a way to work with one another. Organigrams and detailed job descriptions act as makeshift crash barriers, but they leave plenty of space for bitter turf wars to break out—whether that involves taking over more responsibilities or dumping them on someone else ("not my job, mate"). Areas of responsibility not being clearly defined throws additional fuel on the fire.

---

98   "Abschied von der Doppelspitze," *Zeiti*, July 16, 2007, www.zeit.de.
99   "Champagner für den Airbus-Chef," *Neue Zürcher Zeitung*, December 30, 2008, www.nzz.ch.

Employees absorbed in marking out their territory have a tendency to neglect their official duties.

Team Training in the Cockpit: The Crew Coordination Concept

Targeted measures such as team-building seminars are usually introduced only after the horse has bolted and the working environment has become so bad that productivity is being affected. In most cases, tension in the office has both a hard component (Who does what?) and a soft one (How do people get on?). Both of these components need to be tackled. Effective cooperation has been a targeted outcome of training in the aviation industry for many years now. The "Crew Coordination Concept" (CCC) is now a core part of pilot training. How can businesses benefit from this methodology?

A WRENCH IN THE WORKS

Shocking Statistics

Co-workers' inability to cooperate increases the risk of a crash, something that has long been recognized within the aviation industry and beyond. One trade journal noted this liability back in the mid-90s, for example: "According to a study by the US National Transportation Safety Board (NTSB), of 15 air accidents investigated, 11 took place during the first day a captain and co-pilot worked together. In a further 37 air accidents investigated, the NTSB found that a lack of mutual monitoring on the part of the cabin crew contributed to the accident."[100] Findings like these led to the development of the Crew Coordination Concept, which is based primarily three principles.

Guiding Principles of CCC

1. Clear divisions of tasks, competencies, and responsibilities are listed for the cockpit (What does the pilot flying do; what does the pilot not flying do?).
2. Similarly precise instructions for carrying out specific tasks, with individual working steps, are defined in a checklist (standard operating procedures).

---

100 Heinz-Dieter Meier, "Spannungsfeld Cockpit: Crew Coordination," *Rotorblatt*, nos. 1–2 (1996), www.german-helicopter.com.

3. Mutual monitoring by the cabin crew is prescribed. The PF calls from the checklist, and the PNF responds, either confirming or challenging if he considers that the correct course of action in the circumstances is not being applied (closed-loop principle).

Parallel Worlds in Business

The Official—and Unofficial—View

While a crystal clear division of duties and an unambiguous, predetermined communications routine is now par for the course in the cockpit, in the business world in general, "parallel worlds" often exist within a company. Everyone who survives their probation period knows that there is an official org chart, and then there is the real power structure in the company. There are the official channels, and then there are well-trodden shortcuts. On the one hand are working groups, meetings, and decisions; on the other, one finds old-boy networks, connections, and concealed opposition. Some who occupy the uppermost boxes in the org chart fill little more than a sinecure, and many projects pushed with demonstrative enthusiasm can thank their existence largely to political correctness or the desire to keep up with the latest trend, be it "diversity" or "sustainability." Looked at this way, a business, in all its individuality, complexity, and unpredictability, resembles a living organism. Indeed, anything else would be astonishing as one considers human vanity and hunger for power, prejudices and weaknesses, sympathies and antipathies—for none are left behind at the office door.

Quality Management: Controlling Processes

Bringing this proliferating disorder under control with standards and regulations—in the same way that clear rules are insisted upon in the cockpit—is not a new idea. This approach is known simply as "quality management." Processes are defined, described, and made mandatory. Everything is documented, filling filing cabinets and databases. If you just let out a sigh, you are in good company. QM has earned itself a lasting reputation as an information graveyard of limited practical value. In the worst cases, its sole purpose is to allow an impressive-looking logo to be used or to earn the latest "insert acronym" certification. The most beautifully recorded process documentation and the procedural steps derived from it are worth nothing if, after their painstaking production, they are left to yellow in the bottom of a filing cabinet. My recommendation is, therefore, to limit the standards and regulations to the truly critical parts of the business. It really is not too far off the situation in the air; in aviation, checklists and standard operating procedures exist primarily for the riskiest phases—takeoff and landing—and for potential inflight emergencies.

Personality Clashes Causing Conflict

Beyond that, it is a victory in itself if decision makers remain aware that parallel worlds might exist behind the everyday façade of office life and keep a watchful eye out that they do not conflict with the business's or department's official plans. There have been enough cases where hidden agendas and informal power structures have proven their destructive potential. That includes pronounced animosity between decision makers, from the typical disputes between the production and development departments or those working in the office and the field, to trench warfare between individuals (e.g., head of marketing and the commercial director), and up to power struggles right at the top. The further up the structure the hostilities take place, the more damaging their effect can be—EADS being one example. This is even true in traditional family businesses, such as model railway maker Märklin, which was driven into insolvency in part by the bitter feuding of three competing family branches.

Emotional Explosives: How to Defuse

Animosity in the cockpit has endangered many an aircraft. Take the legendary outburst by an African-American co-pilot to his white captain, as the aircraft ran into difficulties: "I'm not doing anything for you, white bitch!" Let us not kid ourselves that the workplace is always going to be a haven of rationality. When the going gets tough, emotions become more intense, particularly destructive emotions. Take action to keep them in check, or you will regret it. Possible courses of action include the following:

- Focusing energy on a common goal (or a common enemy)
- Separating the warring parties
- Making sure interfaces are clearly defined

Questions for the Unofficial World

To get to the bottom of informal structures and power relationships, as a consultant I often pose very simple, but potent, questions:

- What would I (as a newcomer) have to do to get myself fired as quickly as possible?
- Who could make my life difficult if he wanted to, or who is in a position to cause trouble?
- Who would you listen to if you wanted to know whether a project made sense or not?

These, or similar, questions bring the unwritten rules, the informal power relationships, to the light of day. Obviously, you won't need to put these questions to upper management. At that level, nearly everyone is a true believer in the official organigram. Turn to people who are at the coal face; it's the ones at the heart of the system you need to understand.

Sponsored Rivalries

In aviation, the fact that tension in the cockpit is dangerous (because it distracts crew from their primary tasks and hinders successful cooperation, vital in an emergency situation) has informed industry best practice for years. However, the message does not seem to have reached all businesses. On the contrary, in some organizations, rivalries are deliberately encouraged. Divide and rule is often the logic behind it, sometimes the conviction that competition drives efficiency. Two things are being overlooked: first, the energy poured into these turf wars is lost to the business as a whole, and second, once rivalries come to dominate thinking, there is a danger that normal company business will be lost sight of altogether.

ANTI-CRASH FORMULA

To avoid a crash, everyone needs to do his job. Hostilities in the (company) cockpit are dangerous; they distract from the task at hand.

Interaction = Risk

Define Responsibilities

Providing a clear framework for workplace interaction means, above all, to clearly define responsibilities: who does what, and when does another person take over? "Competencies" and "responsibilities" might sound old-fashioned and bureaucratic to some in this open-plan, hot-desking age, but if these formalities are ignored, misunderstandings and conflict will be the inevitable result. One of the reasons for the dramatically reduced number of accidents in civil aviation over the past decades is doubtless the strict definition of "cockpit responsibilities." Here, the question of the definition of individual roles and regulation of interaction naturally intertwine.

Who Writes the Press Release?

One example of the interaction/communication problem: In one large industry trade body, conflict and wasted time are a regular occurrence when press releases and interviews by the association's president need to be prepared. The press officer delegates the task to the relevant department, depending on the subject. In the department responsible for "energy," the same story repeats itself every time. The departmental head is the first to receive the request; then she delegates the task to her personal assistant and to her deputy. The deputy then forwards the task to two or three aides across the office under the heading "Prepare This." Who should prepare or deliver what to whom and when remains shrouded in mystery. The result can be that the same work being done twice or not being done properly at all because nobody feels responsible. Working into the night to get it done at the last minute follows or, alternatively, competing final versions are presented. Misunderstandings about the task at hand are par for the course as there can be many questions over content: Key words? "Tidying up" quotes? Comprehensive background research and detail, or just a short summary? Inevitably, bitterness and disputes about who should be doing what poison the working atmosphere. Every couple of months, everyone decides that the department needs to "optimize workflow." But it never happens.

A Growing Team: More Delegation

The greater the use of delegation within an organization, the more points of contact there are and the greater the need for coordination is. Without the division of labor, the efficiency of the modern economy is unimaginable. At the same time, this division of labor must itself be organized efficiently; otherwise, part of the time and monetary savings it generates will be wasted through coordination difficulties. In new businesses, particularly start-ups set up by young entrepreneurs, this problem is frequently underestimated. In a two-person team, problems can be resolved with a quick word and a handshake, but by the time five people are involved, clear ground rules need to be in place. Company founders often have difficulty coming to terms with this idea; Larry Page and Sergey Brin, for example, delayed three years after founding Google before bringing in Eric Schmidt, an experienced old-school IT manager, as CEO—largely due to pressure from their financial backers.[101] Schmidt was tasked with "building the corporate infrastructure needed to maintain Google's rapid growth as a company," while Page retained responsibility for products and Brin, technology.[102]

Managing Interactions

The best way to ensure that staff interaction runs smoothly is to make sure that everyone knows the following:

- What he is responsible for.
- What exact end product is expected of him, and when it must be ready.
- In what state his end product is to be passed on to the next person in the chain.
- What additional information is required for the handover to ensure that his colleague can take over without any difficulties or misunderstandings.

Ensure Balance

A clear briefing on the one hand and a well-organized handover on the other are the basis of successful coordination management. In both cases, checklists and other documentation can help prevent vital steps being missed and also help avoid

---

101 David A. Vise and Mark Malseed, *The Google Story* (Hamburg: Murmann, 2006).
102 "Google Management," www.google.com.

ambiguity. This is not bureaucratic or uncool; quite simply, it is professional. Impromptu, spontaneous, on-the-hoof arrangements ("Oh, Smith, since you're here, could you just . . .") are notoriously prone to ambiguities, misunderstandings, and mistakes. And since each new interaction needs to be managed successfully, the number of contact points should not be any bigger than absolutely necessary. Put bluntly, the blessings of delegation and the problems of coordination need to be carefully weighed out.

ANTI-CRASH FORMULA

Draw clear boundaries between different areas of responsibility. Formulate clear rules for the handover of work in progress. Use checklists and documentation to avoid misunderstandings and minimize loss of information.

A TRICKY BALANCE: PRESCRIPTION AND PERSONAL RESPONSIBILITY

To make handovers and workload division work all roles of the acting persons have to be clearly defined and separated from each other. For a working crew coordination in the cockpit, besides the division in pilot flying and pilot not flying, it is crucial that everyone knows exactly what the tasks of her role are and that she strictly sticks to and accomplishes them. Everything else could lead to catastrophic results. Also in corporations it should be perfectly clear who is at the controls.

Clearly Defined Roles

The Situation at Automotive Suppliers

Let us start with an example. Automobile parts suppliers have always been exposed to particularly harsh competitive pressures. We discussed this in the previous chapter. The major auto manufacturers rule the market. They pass on their cost pressures, and competition is correspondingly intense among their suppliers. Added to that are the tight deadlines caused by modern production philosophies, such as "just in time." Delivering top quality without delay is essential for economic survival in this sector. That means that any company that does not have complete oversight over its processes is bound to have big problems.

Differing Understanding of Roles . . .

One of my customers was a smaller company which produced bodywork components. As in the previous example, I had been brought in as an advisor, again because many of their processes were failing to gel. Delivery problems and customer complaints were a daily occurrence. Just from the preliminary talks, one significant contributor to the misery soon became clear: the chief executive (who, to make matters worse, was also one of the owners) was quick to complain of an unwillingness to take responsibility and a lack of entrepreneurial spirit among his managers. He wanted them to step up and take the reins themselves. His managers, on the other hand, saw the situation in quite the opposite light; they felt they were lacking clear direction and any overarching vision on the part of their boss.

. . . And the Consequences

This scenario is a classic example of ill-defined roles. Clearly, differing expectations existed of what a chief executive and the level of management directly below him should be doing. Competencies and decision-making authority had not been explicitly defined; instead, certain unspoken assumptions defined expectations. As a result, decisions were delayed and consultation became a weary, drawn-out process. Conditions like these often result from a change in leadership, where a younger manager takes over the reins from an authoritarian, patriarchal boss. The predecessor wanted to run everything personally, while the new guy takes it as a given that his managers will be self-starters.

In aviation, which roles are assigned to whom are documented in voluminous handbooks, meticulously regulated with checklists and standard operating procedures. In business, job descriptions and process chains should at least offer a rough outline. If you want to avoid problems like the ones described above, two important preconditions need to be met:

1. **Everyone in the company knows his role.** *Unambiguous job descriptions are vital.* Clear job descriptions are anything but a given. Human resources may have developed a whole series of tools (requirement profiles, competence models, job descriptions) designed to regulate the duties and responsibilities of workers, from secretary to senior executive, down to the last detail. But the finest tools available are worthless if they are not

used or taken seriously. At the same time, the majority of newly employed workers would be pleased to receive clear instructions as to what their role entails. In practice, being thrown into the deep end is a much more common—and problematic—experience than a systematic induction that includes the clarification of competencies, duties, and responsibilities. It seems that an attitude of letting the "newbie" get on with it, and seeing how he does, is commonplace. The newcomer is left groping in the dark, hoping that he does not do too much damage. An example: The senior partner of a medium-sized family business hired a new chief executive. Following in the footsteps of a lawyer who was retiring after 30 years with the company, he was supposed to be a "breath of fresh air." As the successor got to work making real changes to the company's internal workings, disputes and then dismissal followed. The justification was that the chief executive "constantly exceeded his remit." Only then was it clear who was really pulling the strings in the company and wanted to retain all decision-making authority: the senior partner.

2. **Everyone in the company is genuinely happy with her role.** *Say "yes" to your job.* There is so much you can write on paper. But in real life it is not enough that competencies and responsibilities are written down. There will always be employees who have not truly accepted their responsibility for what, according to the organigram or their job description, they are actually supposed to be doing. One example: The successful salesperson who changes jobs and makes the leap to sales manager. However, at the new company, it soon becomes clear that the structured development of sales strategies and working with budgets is not her forte. The result? She takes refuge in day-to-day business minutiae, spends more time in the field than in the office, visiting clients and getting in the way of her salesforce. The sales department is left rudderless, which is reflected in declining sales figures. And there are also employees who, in contrast, find their role as described too restrictive and attempt to throw their weight around in other areas. An example of this is the graphic designer at a PR agency who is responsible for the optical design and realization of layouts, but who consistently puts up the backs of the copywriters by drawing them into discussions

and attempting to "improve" their work by suggesting a new slogan or choosing the "right" adjective.

Tips for Managers

If you want to avoid such problems among those working for you, you should employ the following methods:

- Create a precise and unambiguous job description for every position, including handover points, competencies, and core duties.
- Ensure that this profile is actually used during the hiring process (in advertising, interviews, and the contract).
- Make certain that everyone within the organization actually knows his own job description.
- Ensure that job profiles are regularly updated.
- Resolve not to operate on the basis of unspoken assumptions; rather, make your key expectations explicitly known to all staff.
- Avoid paying lip service; that is, avoid coming out with platitudes that you do not really stand behind ("big changes," "getting tough," "a new paradigm").

As an employee, you need to demand this clarification. If management does not follow through, at least you know that you are already on thin ice.

ANTI-CRASH FORMULA

Ensure that roles are clearly defined. Everyone in the company needs to know exactly what his core tasks and competencies are. Demand this kind of clarity for yourself too.

Supporting Self-Starters

Working to Plan: No Thanks

"Competencies," "responsibilities," and "core tasks"—these words may have one or two of you thinking of the dead hand of bureaucracy, of working "by the book," and a triumphantly evasive "Sorry, that's not my department." Admittedly, if the majority of people in a business really do *only* fulfil their formal responsibilities, then that company has some problems to attend to. In the day-to-day business environment, it is impossible to plan for all eventualities in advance and regulate them with checklists and job descriptions. Of course, that is what makes "working to plan" such a bogeyman for managers as well as customers.

Not My Job, Mate

The absurd consequences of someone stubbornly refusing to do more than what is "nailed down" in his job description is neatly illustrated by Reinhard K. Sprenger in *The Principle of Responsibility*. He uses the example of a gardener, raking leaves in a shopping center parking lot. His rake is missing half its tines. A senior manager who happened to be inspecting the store that day sees him and asks him why he is using this old rake; it's going to take him all day. The stoic answer: "They gave me this rake." Why he did not get another rake? Answer: "That's not my job." The manager decided to find the gardener's line manager and impress upon him the need to ensure all staff have the proper equipment.[103]

The Solution: The Golden (Leadership) Mean

Rightly, at this point, Sprenger warns of a "completely excessive conception of leadership." Is it really a line manager's job to check that his team members' equipment is in perfect working order on a regular basis? I believe that his real role is to lead his team in such a manner that team members will think to sort it out themselves. The instruction, "Before you start work, count the tines on your rake," should not have to be written into the job profile. In over 15 years as a consultant, I have become acquainted with dozens of businesses and worked intensively with countless managers. In my experience during this time, there seem to be two basic tendencies: either leadership is extremely controlling and inflexible (motto: "If you want a job properly, do it yourself") or extremely lax (motto: "That's what we pay these people for"). Only rarely does one encounter the golden mean between authoritarian leadership and rudderless laissez-faire in real life—even though, officially at least, "cooperative leadership" is trumpeted

---

103 Reinhard K. Sprenger, *Das Prinzip Selbstverantwortung* (The Principle of Personal Responsibility) (Frankfurt: Campus, 2005), 9.

as the model for successful management. The crux of the matter is this: anyone who wants employees who think for themselves must avoid both over- and undermanaging.

Warning: Micromanagement

In the case of "overmanagement," the reason is plain to see: superiors who micromanage their workers (standing over their shoulders here, grabbing the controls themselves there) will in the long or short run instill feelings of resignation and apathy. Think of the co-pilot mentioned in the first example. After numerous interventions by the captain, and without consciously thinking about it, he mentally surrendered his job to his superior. For his part, the captain presumably believed that he was just "helping" here and there, and besides, the co-pilot would do his job as pilot flying quite automatically. Warning bells for such cases of resignation in business include claims such as "No one wants you to think here" or "What does it matter when they complain whatever you do?" To this day, there are companies in which all incoming mail lands on the desk of the owner and leaves it, in the case of the most critical matters at any rate, "helpfully" covered with annotations and instructions. This principle is reflected in the endemic "cc" mania that blights email communication; if the boss reads it too, then he'll surely chime in if he's not happy with something. A manager who promotes or even demands this variety of "delegation" of responsibility has no right to be surprised if work grinds to a halt in his absence.

A Shocking Exercise

Controlling behavior and micromanagement infantilizes employees and, in the long run, leads to defiance and resistance. Paradoxically, undermanagement can have the same effect—at least when it is coupled with excessive demands. An employee who feels abandoned with an impossible(for him) workload, fearing that he will never be able to get on top of it whatever he does, will also lose all motivation. In the worst case, he will simply give up. In my seminars, I sometimes use a simple exercise to illustrate this. Participants throw rubber balls to each other, attempting to reach a certain number of exchanges as quickly as possible. The groups try it for a while and gradually improve their efficiency.

Unrealistic Targets Demotivate

In this illustration, at some point, when a round can be completed in about two minutes, I tell everyone that the fastest group managed it in less than 12 seconds—which is true, but de facto incomprehensible for the participants. The target is so extreme and so far beyond the realms of plausibility that each time, the same fascinating process takes place: after a few minutes, the first few start to quit, protesting ("I've had enough of this nonsense!") and stalling; the smokers suddenly need to have a cigarette before they can do anything else. It does not take long before the entire group refuses to carry on (depending on the dominant temperament, either sullenly silent or fuming with unconcealed anger). There could hardly be a better way to demonstrate to managers the futility of setting impossible targets. Demanding a 20 percent increase in turnover when 7 or 8 percent would be an ambitious target does not automatically lead to employees giving their all. If you are unlucky, they will give up halfway, refuse to continue, or even openly call your judgment into question.

Warning: Undermanagement

The effect is similar when managers let employees do as they will, effectively abandoning their own role as leaders. Frequently, these are conflict-avoidant personalities and people who could never get used to a leadership role (like the salesperson above). Up to a point, employees will do their best to manage on their own. If the feeling grows that whatever they do, they have no hope of succeeding, resignation sets in. Mentally, they have already handed in their notice: "I can't make a difference anyway."

Sharing Responsibility

Taking responsibility, in contrast, means being proactive. Even without the helping hand of explicit instructions and regulations, responsibility takes action because the situation demands it, because I am capable of doing it. If I am constantly put under too much pressure, or conversely left with little to do and no sense of agency; if I constantly have my work interfered with or have to comply with restrictive guidelines; if I lack the necessary support, then, almost inevitably, I will struggle to act on my own initiative. Given this reality, good leadership means providing orientation and making roles and duties crystal clear, creating the conditions in which workers can be successful independently. Simplified, one might say, "Give your employees as much responsibility as they can deal with." In practical terms, that means not only delegating tasks and activities, but also responsibility. Responsibility means the opportunity to act freely within a given framework—indeed, to decide and do what they think is right. This remains true even when you, as an outsider, "know how to do it better" (in your specialist area, for example). If you want your team to truly accept responsibility, then *you* must genuinely relinquish responsibility to them, in deed and not just word.

ANTI-CRASH FORMULA

If you want your employees to take responsibility, let them "get on with it" as far as their potential (within a satisfactory definition of roles) allows.

ASSIGNING WORK PROFESSIONALLY

So much has already been said about leadership and motivation that it can sometimes feel like there is nothing left to say. Nevertheless, I consider it helpful to take another look at such important topics in regards to efficiently delegating work.

Bite-Sized Delegation

The Trainee Pilot Learns Step by Step

When a flying instructor is teaching someone how to pilot an aircraft, you will never hear him say anything along the lines of, "You land for a change today. You'll have to do it sooner or later; no time like the present! Well, what are you waiting for? Go ahead!" That could well prove to be a risky and bumpy business. An experienced instructor will, instead, entrust his pupil with just as much as he can be expected to manage while remaining fully focused. So first of all, a controlled descent in planned stages will be practiced, and only when the student has mastered that will he be trusted to land the plane himself. While the inexperienced student practices the descent, responsibility for everything else lies with the instructor.

Situational Leadership

The appropriate delegation of tasks by managers looks very similar. Delegating correctly will prevent employees being given either too much or too little to deal with; the ideal is to give them just enough freedom for the task to remain challenging and motivating. The appropriate amount to delegate in individual cases depends on the experience and expertise of the employee concerned and on the complexity of the task. The "situational leadership" model is an attempt to identify this happy medium by dividing workers into four categories.

Employee Categories

1. Employees who are very capable and motivated → "Delegate" (Let them take on a large amount of responsibility.)
2. Employees who are capable but unwilling → "Support" (Avoid micromanagement; praise highly; offer moral support.)
3. Employees who are have little ability and are unwilling → "Train" (Provide equal amounts of direction and praise.)
4. Employees who are unable but motivated → "Direct" (Direct and oversee.)[104]

Doubts about the Categories

It is certainly worth drawing attention to flexible leadership styles, which have to be adapted to the respective situation. Nevertheless, I regard these pseudo-precise categories with a certain degree of skepticism. In my experience, people are not so easy to categorize and, above all, cannot be permanently assigned to one box or other. Besides, this model does not take all possibilities into account. What happens, for example, when capability and motivation are both equally low?

Delegate in "Chunks"

Instead of pigeonholing employees, I encourage managers to take each case on its merits and only then assign the task that the employee will be responsible for. How much can he carry right now? Do you need to ease the burden (further)? In IT,

---

104 Kenneth Blanchard and Patricia Zigarmi and Dea Zigarmi, *Der Minuten-Manager* (The One Minute Manager) (Reinbek near Hamburg: Rowohlt, 2005).

the expression "chunks" is used to describe the amount of information that can be successfully processed.

Delegating the right size of chunk is, in my experience, one of the secrets of successful leadership. Give your employee as much as he can manage: no more and no less. Here, specialist knowledge, practical experience, workload, and also psychological factors play a role. If someone is suffering from personal problems, he will not be the go-to person for an ambitious project. And the eagerly ambitious will have a different approach to a new project than someone who has been counting the days to early retirement.

To measure the chunk out correctly, you need to show an interest in your employees, to know and speak to them. That sounds more banal than it is. In practice, a sizeable minority of managers treat this core competency of management as a burden. In practical terms, you should employ the following techniques when delegating.

Rules for Delegation
- Plan ahead what might be delegated; create clearly defined chunks.
- Make it clear what completion of the task involves. Define what result you are expecting, and when you expect it.
- Ask the employee if he feels his skillset matches the task.
- Give responsibility for the task to the employee.
- Clarify which areas remain your responsibility, what you wish to be kept informed of, and under what circumstances you will intervene.
- Avoid "boomerang delegation" by offering to help if problems develop; rather, *let him get on with it*. Avoid doing it for him. For many managers, this is the hardest part.
- Once the task is completed, ask the employee how difficult he found it.
- Give him hot feedback on how well he completed the task from your point of view.

Responsibilities Made Clear
It should be absolutely clear throughout the process who is responsible for what. This keeps misunderstandings to a minimum and empowers employees to work with freedom. Motivation and a high level of engagement should be a precondition.

Simply avoiding *de*motivating employees can be an achievement in itself. And however much "recognition" you give to them, the value system of people who view their work as a tiresome burden is not going to change.

ANTI-CRASH FORMULA

Delegating correctly calls for clearness and precision. What is the employee responsible for? What do you expect from him and when? What do you take responsibility for yourself?

Critical Areas Unambiguous

One thing will certainly be clear to you by now: it is impossible to plan for every contingency that might occur at work and be ready to combat it with checklists and action plans. And it is not necessary either, if you can rely on your staff to act independently. For areas where problems and neglect could have devastating consequences, however, it certainly is worth maintaining strict guidelines. This is another concept one can learn from civil aviation, where clear guidelines are always in place for problematic situations. Consider the following example.

Historic Glide

August 2001 witnessed the longest glide by a jet aircraft in the history of aviation to that date. An Air Transat plane heading from Toronto to Lisbon lost power in both engines and was forced to make an emergency landing in the Azores. With fuel exhausted, the last 75 miles to Terceira Island were made in a glide. Of 306 people on board, a couple were injured during the evacuation of the aircraft on the ground, but no one was killed. The pilots were celebrated as heroes. Ironically, although the flying skills demonstrated by the cockpit crew were certainly impressive, if they had followed the emergency checklist procedure as they should have done, no heroics would have been called for. They would have had plenty of fuel to reach the airport.

How the Fuel Ran Out

The cause of the fuel loss was a leak in the starboard engine of the Airbus A330. This set off a warning chime, which the crew dismissed as a false alarm at first. An imbalance between the left and right fuel tanks forced them to confront the problem. The crew started pumping fuel from the tank in the left wing into the tank in the right wing—in effect, directly into the leak. This unnecessarily accelerated the rate of fuel loss. At 6:13 a.m., the first engine cut out, and the second cut out 13 minutes later. At 6:45 a.m., they landed relatively safely at Lajes Air Base. The investigation by Portuguese aviation authorities noted tersely, "Conducting the Fuel Imbalance procedure by memory negated the defense of the Caution note in the Fuel Imbalance checklist that may have caused the crew to consider timely actioning of the Fuel Leak procedure . . . Not actioning the Fuel Leak procedure was the key factor that led to the fuel exhaustion."[105]

Sensitive Parts of the Business

In every business, there are sensitive areas where a major problem would endanger the whole company. These reach from reliable scheduling and up-to-date know-how in information services to hygiene in a restaurant and compliance in an investment bank. Anyone who cannot get to meetings on time and cannot be relied on to solve customer problems will soon have no customers at all. Anyone who violates food safety standards risks having his restaurant shut down by health inspectors. And if the compliance team of a financial services company fails to identify legal risks and to oversee compliance with national and international laws (against fraud, insider trading, or money laundering, for example), legal action, eye-watering fines, and a PR disaster can result.

Is there a section of your company where things going wrong would prove disastrous? Where do working processes have to be perfectly structured and solid results guaranteed? Where have you sometimes thought to yourself, "Whew, that just worked out this time"—but did nothing to avoid a similar situation recurring?

ANTI-CRASH FORMULA

What are the critical areas in your business? Where must problems be avoided at all costs? Have you planned ahead and prepared precise instructions and checklists?

---

105 "Accident Investigation Final Report: All Engines-out Landing due to Fuel Exhaustion. Air Transat Airbus A330-243 Marks C-GITS. Lajes, Azores, Portugal. August 24, 2001," www.moptc.pt/templfiles/200608181643moptc.pdf.

The Closed-Loop Principle: No Room for Misunderstanding

The Closed Loop in Civil Aviation

In the cockpit, the pilot announces every step taken, and the PNF either confirms or explicitly challenges. To facilitate this, pilot training drills firm, unmistakable "standard calls." For example, a change of course, turning right heading north, would sound like this: the PF says, "Turning right; heading 360." The PNF observes the actions of his colleague flying the plane. If the aircraft has indeed changed heading, as announced, and is facing north, the PNF answers, "360 is checked." This principle of mutual monitoring and observation is termed the "closed-loop principle." The clearly regulated feedback mechanism maximizes safety. Do both crew members perceive the situation in the same way? Is the pilot flying reacting adequately to the situation?

The Business Dialect

Closed-loop introduces redundancy into the communication as information is double-checked. This helps avoid misunderstandings that could have fatal consequences. The jargon common in many businesses is light years away from this simple unambiguity. As the *Frankfurter Allgemeine Zeitung* once put it, a "bloated mixture of say-nothing surgically spliced Anglo-German hybrids and adventurous sentence structure" is typical for many a German business. A taster: "A process cost evaluation was carried out, and we are undertaking cost plausibility assessment through the use of theoretical price calculations. The progress of the project is being monitored through the use of quality gates."[106] OK. Got that?

Hoping that people will start calling a spade a spade when the business runs into difficulties is nothing more than whistling in the wind. Graduates unleashed on the real world with a vocabulary gleaned from business studies textbooks and marketing jargon often know no better. And indeed, this jargon is often wonderfully suited to inflating middling ideas into imposing visions or casting a verbal shroud around personal mediocrity. This is exactly what makes it so dangerous—the distancing effect soothes when urgent action is called for. The company might be on the brink of collapse, and in the next meeting,

---

106 Markus Reiter, "Managersprache: Wild wucherndes Wirtschaftskauderwelsch," *Frankfurter Allgemeine Zeitung*, July 29, 2006, www.faz.net.

"negative growth" will be calmly announced and a philosophical debate over black or red zeros conducted.

Sayings and Their (Real) Meaning

Added to this is the fact that language isn't always clear; it lies open to interpretation. Each of us operates with hundreds of indirect hints, insinuations, and unspoken expectations every day. We say, "That will increase costs," yet mean, "We can't afford that in these circumstances." We say, "That's a topic for the agenda for next Wednesday," yet mean, "This idea is so potentially risky that I won't pursue it without covering my back with upper management first." We say, "We don't have the capacity to do that at the moment," yet maybe we mean, "You'll need to take care of that yourself."

Of course, day-to-day business communication cannot be reduced to a few fixed expressions. But when the going does get tough, you need to keep the pitfalls of human communication in mind. It is better to make sure than risk being misunderstood. There are a few trusty expressions that can help you achieve "verbal insurance."

Verbal Insurance

- What does that mean exactly?
- Do you mean to say that . . . ?
- Who is doing what? Are you taking care of . . . ?
- When exactly will it be done?
- If I understand you correctly, that means . . . ?
- What does that mean in practice? What's the next step?
- You expect me to do . . . And in the meantime, you take care of . . . ?
- Put simply, that means the next steps are 1 . . . 2 . . . 3 . . . Am I right?

ANTI-CRASH FORMULA

Make an effort to get communicative feedback. In tricky situations, use the closed-loop principle.

UNCERTAIN BOUNDARIES—AND WHAT YOU CAN DO

Ensuring clear communication is one of the first and most decisive steps to professional crisis management. In conclusion, here once again, at a glance, are the most important methods for ensuring a transparent division of roles and responsibilities.

ANTI-CRASH FORMULAS AT A GLANCE

1. To avoid a crash, everyone needs to do his job. Hostilities in the (company) cockpit are dangerous; they distract from the task at hand.
2. Draw clear boundaries between different areas of responsibility. Formulate clear rules for the handover of work in progress. Use checklists and documentation to avoid misunderstandings and minimize loss of information.
3. Ensure that roles are clearly defined. Everyone in the company needs to know exactly what his core tasks and competencies are. Demand this kind of clarity for yourself too.
4. If you want your employees to take responsibility, let them "get on with it" as far as their potential (within a satisfactory definition of roles) allows.
5. Delegating correctly calls for clearness and precision. What is the employee responsible for? What do you expect from him and when? What do you take responsibility for yourself?
6. What are the critical areas in your business? Where must problems be avoided at all costs? Have you planned ahead and prepared precise instructions and checklists?
7. Make an effort to get communicative feedback. In tricky situations, use the closed-loop principle.

CHAPTER 6

BLAME CULTURE

(Or When Mistakes Are Covered Up)

+ + + July 8, 1987 + + + A Delta Air Lines plane veers off course over the North Atlantic. + + + Result: collision at 30,000 feet avoided by a matter of seconds. + + + 589 passengers lucky to suffer nothing worse than a shock. + + +

Two fully occupied passenger planes on a deadly collision course over the middle of the Atlantic? A nightmare scenario, but one that came close to being reality in the summer of 1987. It was pure luck that nearly 600 passengers and crew were spared a midair collision, by a hair's breadth. Both aircraft, a Delta Lockheed L-1011 and a Continental 747, had taken off from London Gatwick that afternoon towards the United States. Thanks to information being incorrectly entered into the Lockheed's navigation system, its autopilot steered it 60 miles off course—without the pilots realizing. At 16:25, their jet crossed the flight path of the 747 at a distance of only 20 meters. At speeds of almost 600 miles per hour, it was no more than the blink of an eye. No less shocking than the incident itself was the behavior of the Delta crew afterwards: they attempted to cover the mistake up. It was brought to light by frightened Continental passengers. They had witnessed the other aircraft racing towards them. Their protests forced their flight crew to report the incident.[107]

LEARNING FROM MISTAKES

They say that those who don't learn from their mistakes are doomed to repeat them. The airline industry has taken this lesson to heart. For decades, the systematic review of all incidents has been obligatory. Every crash is meticulously analyzed, and incidents like the near-miss must be reported to the authorities. The findings are then fed back into pilot training and training programs designed to enhance safety levels, like Crew Resource Management. Mistakes are dealt with—provided, of course, that the "human factor" doesn't get in the way.

Dealing with Mistakes: Theory and Practice

Assessing failures and accidents this thoroughly would, of course, be of great value in "normal" branches of the economy, quite apart from such safety-critical industries as air, nuclear, and chemical. The concept of mistakes being "learning opportunities" is now firmly established, and whenever managers get together, it doesn't take long for a consensus to emerge that a "no-blame culture" is good for business. That's all very well as far as the theory goes. As regards practice, as business psychologist and researcher of error training Professor Michael Frese put it, "High-quality research has been conducted into the question of how different cultures and countries deal with failure. Of 61 different countries in the analysis, Germany was

---

107 Richter and Wolf, 63.

second to last, ahead of Singapore." In other words, Germany actually has one of the strongest "blame cultures" in the world.[108]

Germany's "Error Culture"

From earliest childhood, we all learned that it is wrong to make mistakes. If we made mistakes in school, we got bad grades. Our friends would make fun of us, and our parents would punish us. People who don't make mistakes get on. Companies boast of applying "zero defect" standards. Mistakes are simply embarrassing. And now, at work, we are supposed to just push all this experience to one side, flip a switch, and be able to deal "constructively" with mistakes (including our own)? You can be forgiven for having your doubts.

CRASH EXAMPLE: NORTH ATLANTIC, JUNE 1987

If Germany's highly respected current affairs magazine *Der Spiegel* can be believed, then the Delta crew's reaction to the incident was about as responsible and professional as an eight-year-old caught by his peers swiping apples. "Nobody knows about it except us, you idiots!" was said to have been their charming rejoinder to the crew of the Continental plane, who had requested they report the incident.[109]

The Buildup to the Near Miss

What exactly was going on? The plane had taken off from London Gatwick in the early afternoon, headed for Cleveland, Ohio—just one of many aircraft crossing the Atlantic towards North America that day. For the ocean crossing, airliners are assigned an air corridor that corresponds to a certain latitude. These "tracks" are 60 miles apart and are designed to keep planes at a comfortably safe distance. At the time, airliners used an inertial navigation system (INS), whose data also fed into the autopilot. For the first two and a half hours of the flight, everything ran smoothly. Then, at 16:06, the autopilot suddenly made a disastrous course correction. Instead of making a gentle 10 degree turn to the left, it changed the plane's course by more than 35 degrees. Unnoticed by the crew, the Lockheed had left its corridor. It is not hard to imagine how fast things go traveling at 600 miles

---

108 Wolf Lotter, "Fehlanzeige," *Brand eins*, no. 8 (2007): 51.
109 "Luftfahrt: Modell Schimpanse. Eine Serie von Luftfahr-Zwischenfällen schockte US-Fluggäste" (Aviation: Model Chimpanzee. A Series of Aviation Incidents Shocks US Passengers), *Der Spiegel*, no. 30 (1987): 151, http://wissen.spiegel.de.

per hour in a corridor 60 miles wide. A Continental Airlines plane was flying on the track directly to the south.

Cause: A Slip of the Finger

In the cockpits of both planes, everything seemed like business as usual. Yet catastrophe was drawing nearer with every passing second. At 16:25, passengers looking out of the starboard side windows of the 747 were greeted with the sight of another passenger plane. No one was concerned at first; in fact, someone took a snapshot (the photograph would soon be reproduced in newspapers all over the world). The passengers only started to become uneasy when they realized that the other plane was not only flying at the same altitude as them, but it was also getting closer and closer, at speed. The next second, the Lockheed crossed the 747's path—fortuitously, 20 meters below it. It was only then that the crew in the Delta cockpit noticed the huge shadow directly above them. And this terrifying near miss sprang from a laughably simple mistake: programming the INS at Gatwick, the Delta Air Lines pilot had mixed his numbers up.

Attempted Cover-Up

"The crew of Delta Flight 37 did not report the incident to air traffic control at Gander, the closest airport in Canada. Other crews in the area, who had heard the whole exchange over short-wave radio, also failed to report the incident, although this should have been mandatory. They couldn't bring themselves to 'betray' a glaring error made by one of their own to a third party," remarked Jan-Arwed Richter in *Mayday!*[110] In his account, the incident only came to public light thanks to the Continental crew. Their hand was forced by their own passengers, who were calling the safety of the route into question; they felt they no longer had any choice but to report the incident. *Der Spiegel* also claimed that a USAF plane had recorded the exchange and informed the authorities.[111]

Admitting Mistakes: Without Being Punished

What stops people from speaking up when things go wrong? They say in Brazil that we defend our own mistakes, yet we prosecute those of others. The Bible warned

---

110 Richter and Wolf, 68.
111 "Aviation: Model Chimpanzee," ibid.

us that we see "the mote in our brother's eye sooner than the beam in our own."[112] However cool and considered we might like to think we are, when the shit hits the fan, we prefer saving face to facing up to what we might have done wrong. Indeed, can you remember a manager (especially at the highest level) ever owning up to a mistake? When you was the last time *you* admitted to getting things wrong? And how do you deal with mistakes made by your co-workers? There is only one way to deal with mistakes productively: learn from them. And that will only be possible in your business when workers can speak up when things do go wrong, without fear of suffering for it. In the aviation industry, this is known as the "non-punishment reporting system."

CRASH WARNING

To avoid mistakes in the future, talk through past mistakes. Does your company have a non-punishment reporting system?

COMPANY EXAMPLE: THE WORLD ECONOMIC CRISIS—BLAMING THE BANKERS

Popular Anger Unleashed

"Jump! You fuckers!" The sign held aloft by enraged bank customers on Wall Street was unequivocal. "Eat the bankers," was the rallying cry of protestors in London in 2009. Demonstrators in Frankfurt showed a sense of irony, collecting donations in front of the Deutsche Bank skyscrapers in tins marked "Bread for the bank." The popular German tabloid *Bild* laid claim to the popular mood in accustomed style in March of that year. Depicting the senior management of Dresdner Bank (who, despite needing a government bailout, were to receive a combined €58 million in bonuses, pensions, and golden handshakes) on the front page, it slammed them with the headline "GREEDY BASTARDS." Politicians from across the political spectrum jumped in, with Chancellor Angela Merkel remarking that "earnings have to be earned." And the chairman of the center-left SPD called bankers "Hooligans, pyromaniacs, gangsters."[113] The evening news was filled with outraged

112 Matthew 7:3.

113 Dorothea Siems, "Schuldfrage: Die Manager sind die Sündenböcke der Finanzkrise" (The Question of Guilt: Managers are the Scapegoats of the Financial Crisis), *Die Welt*, May 10,

bank customers, who accused their financial advisors of recklessly destroying six-figure family savings by pushing Lehman certificates on them.

Take a Closer Look

This anger is understandable, but when politicians and consumers place the entirety of the blame for the losses on greedy bankers and financial speculation, they are taking the easy way out. Instead of looking for scapegoats and rushing to provide multi-billion-euro bailouts, it might be more productive to pose some of the following questions: Is it a good idea to invest in financial products that you barely understand (or indeed, can't understand at all)? Is it a good idea to put blind faith in promised returns? Is a properly functioning regulatory system in place for the financial industry? How did such massive problems remain hidden for so long? If you look into the origins of the financial crisis, you will see that the list of "culprits" is a long one.

A Long List: Those to Blame for the Financial Crisis

- The US government, which by federal law compelled banks to lend money to low-income borrowers (Community Reinvestment Act).
- The Federal Reserve, which at the same time flooded the financial markets with cheap money.
- American bankers, who accepted the money with open arms and made endless NINJA loans: no income, no job, no assets.
- American house buyers, who bought houses on credit that they couldn't really afford.
- Investment bankers, who repackaged subprime loans into securities that removed them from the balance sheets.
- The American legal system, who let homeowners simply return their keys to the bank if they could no longer pay the mortgage—and let them off the hook.
- Regional banks in Germany that wanted to be world players and eagerly threw their hats, and assets, into the ring.
- German politicians, who promoted market deregulation, allowing banks to build up enormous debts.

2009, www.welt.de.

- German bankers, who created investment vehicles that, at the end of the day, even they themselves probably only partially understood.
- Executives, who agreed to a bonus system based on turning a quick profit rather than promoting long-term economic stability.
- Customers who put blind faith in bankers and financial advisors in their quest for higher returns and put their money into obscure new investment vehicles.

Why Mistakes Are Glossed Over

Who exactly was being greedy here, greedy for bonuses, for votes, for quick financial gains? Who was naïve, unscrupulous, and reckless? The list confirms two things. First, mistakes are rarely one-offs. For a genuine "perfect storm," certain conditions have to be met (this holds for the airline industry too), mostly caused by an entire series of mistakes, an error chain. Second, pointing the finger of blame at others—without facing up to the mistakes you made yourself—seems to be a basic human reflex. This type of behavior has a psychological and a tactical component. You distance yourself from your own failures and place all the blame on the "other." After all, playing the victim is a lot easier than taking responsibility. *Der Spiegel* magazine noted the story of a top Lehman Brothers banker, who denied any personal responsibility for the company's problems, placing all the blame squarely on upper management: "The fact of the matter is, *eight people* ruined an institution where 20,000 people did good work and made a decent living."[114] In all probability, he truly believed what he was saying.

Strategic Arguments

In many contexts, this kind of behavior is not only psychologically perfectly understandable, it is also good strategy. A politician who wants to be re-elected will do better by minimizing the political contribution to the crisis and instead loudly calling the bankers to account. And a manager who wants to get on will generally behave in just the same way. Who is going to admit to having made a mistake or having neglected part of his duties, when that could mean inviting disciplinary action? Yet in these circumstances, dealing with mistakes positively, with a no-blame culture, becomes an impossibility.

---

114 Beat Balzli, "Der Erreger lebt weiter," *Der Spiegel,* no. 38 (2009): 108, here 113.

WHAT IS A NO-BLAME CULTURE?

To Err Is Human

Hundreds of thousands of words have been expended on failure culture. The journalist Wolf Lotter managed to capture the essentials in just four sentences: "To err is human. So is craziness. Nothing ventured, nothing gained. Only a fool believes he is perfect."[115] A judgmental error culture assumes that mistakes are fundamentally unacceptable and must be avoided at any price. In doing so, such a culture simply ignores human fallibility. That leads to mistakes being swept under the carpet—and also leads to people being afraid to abandon tried and tested methods and try anything new, for fear of making mistakes. If your aim is a positive error culture, you must first accept that mistakes will *always* be made—a challenging task on its own.

A Positive Corporate Culture Is a Prerequisite to Dealing with Mistakes Positively

How Airbus Dealt with Mistakes

Once again, the story behind the Airbus A380 serves as a wonderful example of how large corporations deal with mistakes. Final delivery was being pushed back again and again. The parent company, EADS, was threatened with financial ruin. One of the main reasons for the delays in the $12 billion project was not a highly complex technical problem, but a shockingly simple one: some cables were too short. Each of these superjumbos requires more than 300 miles of wiring for the electronics, lighting, the kitchen, and so on. Any alteration to the plane's interior fittings (slightly adjusting the position of the kitchen, for example, or fitting Internet access) brings a whole series of adjustments to the wiring system in its wake. And this was where communications in the giant corporation broke down. Journalist Christiane Sommer assessed the culture of the multinational company as being plagued by rivalry and mistrust: "No one would admit to a problem as long as the slightest chance remained of fixing it themselves without attracting attention." Management glossed over problems. One insider remarked, "Warning signals would be coming from workers on the front line, and middle managers would just

---

115 Wolf Lotter, "Fehlanzeige," *Brand eins,* no. 8 (2007): 44.

report upwards that everything was running smoothly."[116] In an environment like this, who will be prepared to demand that mistakes be dealt with openly and seen as learning opportunities? To do so would simply be naïve.

Prerequisite: Get the Company Culture Right

Attempting to establish a positive error culture within a destructive corporate culture is an undertaking of roughly the same level of optimism as planting a bed of roses in a dung heap and hoping to enjoy the smell. No one is going to draw attention to his own mistakes if doing so can only be to his disadvantage—from receiving a dressing-down from his line manager to concrete penalties affecting wages, bonuses, and promotion prospects. If everyone tries to keep up the appearance of perfection, and only those who can maintain this façade and show no weakness get ahead, then you have little choice other than to play along. The framework of a positive error culture needs to be compatible with the culture of the business as a whole.

The Advantages of the Toyota Production System

The Toyota Production System (TPS) is often cited as a shining example of how to deal constructively with errors. TPS readily associates with concepts like kaizen and continuous improvement and is given much of the credit for the automaker's success. For one thing, TPS rests on a different assumption than the one present in many Western businesses: that mistakes are undesirable, yet unavoidable. They are accepted as a fact of life and work, and tied into a process of step-by-step improvement in all areas. At same time, we shouldn't lose sight of the fact that a completely different understanding of the worker's role, a different culture, in fact, lies at the heart of this philosophy. Anyone can bring the production lines to a halt if he feels he has reason to, and—regardless of his position in the hierarchy—his contribution to the success of the business will be taken seriously. This is a completely different situation than in Germany, where workers making suggestions for improvement has been *tolerated* for more than a century, but where only a third of the suggestions are actually put into practice. "And not because they had been looked into and found wanting, but because the experts thought, hey, some idiot mechanic or electrician has nothing to say to *me*," as Professor Theo Wehner

---

116 Christiane Sommer, "Verkabelt II. Ein Zwölf-Milliarden-Dollar Projekt droht wegen zu kurzer Kabel zu scheitern. Wie konnte das passieren?" *Brand eins,* no. 3 (2008): 90, here 91.

(whose work includes the study of the psychology of errors) of ETH Zürich wryly remarked.[117]

ANTI-CRASH FORMULA

Dealing with mistakes positively (a no-blame culture) requires a corporate culture that is open, fair, and based on mutual respect; a no-blame culture is one that accepts mistakes are a normal part of the working day.

A Fish Rots from the Head

Managers Are Role Models

Do you remember the Crossair plane that crashed near Zurich in 2001, because the pilot knowingly and systematically flew underneath the minimum permitted altitude in poor visibility and crashed into a forest? The investigation into the crash also revealed that the airline as a whole was ruled by a cavalier attitude to safety and, apparently, the board even endorsed risky maneuvers by their pilots as a token of flying ability (see chapter 3). It is a truism that the culture of a business takes its lead from those at the top. And the relationship is just the same where it comes to dealing with laxity and failures. Why should the "average" investment banker put on sackcloth and ashes when, at the same time, the chairman of the board is suing to get hold of his golden handshake—even though he was responsible for billions in losses?

Prerequisite: Admitting Your Own Mistakes

This doesn't just apply to banks. Senior management covering up its mistakes is one of the best ways to start driving a company to the wall. One example from my experience as a consultant is that of a German company that produced accessories for the furniture industry. The company had been in trouble for a long time, and its backers were beginning to worry about their investment. One of the bankers responsible tasked me with systematically improving the business's negotiating capabilities. The context: one of the main causes for the company's financial difficulties was that it wasn't getting realistic prices for its products. Only part of the

---

117 Lotter.

blame could be put on the market situation; the real kicker was that the business was all too ready to make excessive concessions during negotiations. I suggested that the first step should be a one-day workshop with senior management, in order to get to the root of the problem and explore other ways of negotiating.

Everyone seemed completely convinced—officially at least. However, chances are, managers would have had to confess to their own failures. Undesirability sired impossibility; management found a way—often using some extremely creative logic—to get the event canceled. To this day, the company flirts with bankruptcy on an annual basis; clearly, nothing has been done to improve their disastrous negotiating style. You can probably imagine how well calls for change made by management go down when the managers themselves believe they are untouchable.

Setting an Example

Anyone who wants to change for the better will have to face up to his past mistakes at some point. As a rule, workers have a very keen eye for what "the bosses" get wrong, even if only because we see others' mistakes rather more clearly than we see our own. If the impression takes hold that management doesn't face up to its mistakes, tries to make excuses, or even looks for scapegoats, then, quite understandably, the inclination of the rest of the workforce to be open about their own mistakes tends towards zero.

ANTI-CRASH FORMULA

Whether or not mistakes can genuinely be treated as "learning opportunities" depends to a great extent on the way managers deal with their own mistakes.

TYPES OF MISTAKES, STRINGS OF ERRORS: KNOWING WHAT TO LOOK OUT FOR

IATA Classification as an Incentive

In the airline industry, a serious incident puts human life at risk. Consequently, investigations into incidents can take months and fill filing cabinets. Investigating the root causes of errors in this painstaking way is unlikely to be possible in a normal business context and isn't really necessary in the vast majority of cases.

What can be of use, though, is the accident classification system developed by the International Air Transport Association (IATA), the airline industry's trade body.

Not All Mistakes Are the Same

The IATA categorizes errors into technical, organizational, environmental, and human. The "human" category is subdivided into three different types of mistake: conscious action, unwitting action, and incompetence.

Conscious Action: Active Mistakes

In this instance, someone is actively and consciously breaking known rules and regulations. One example is pilots not completing checklists, which are required for the aircraft to fly safely, or flying below the minimum safe altitude. It is also not completely unheard of for pilots to turn up to work drunk.

Unwitting Action: Passive Mistakes

Here, someone is doing something wrong without being aware of it—acting without due care or without having thought things through; he is unaware of the possible consequences. This might include pilots who don't make the urgency of a situation clear enough when communicating with the tower, who are distracted by visitors to the cockpit, or who simply try to carry on as usual when caution would be advised (for example, ice building up on control surfaces after delays or water on the runway) because their first thought is "Hey, it'll work out."

Incompetence: Proficiency Failures

This is where someone inadvertently makes a mistake because he simply cannot do any better or lacks the knowledge to do it better. This can be due to inexperience, lack of practice, or lack of training. A doubling of near-misses in US airspace in the mid-80s was traced back to the fact that liberalization of the domestic air industry had greatly increased competition, leading to increased numbers of inexperienced pilots sitting at the controls. One old hand called it the "chimpanzee model": the pilots would know what button to press in normal circumstances, but in an emergency, they would be completely out of their depth.[118]

---

118 "Luftfahrt: Modell Schimpanse" (Aviation: Model Chimpanzee), *Der Spiegel*, no. 30 (July 20, 1987), http://wissen.spiegel.de.

Where Training Can Help

A measured approach to failure takes the severity of the mistake into account. If someone makes mistakes due to inexperience and gaps in his understanding, then he needs training. Encouragement is more appropriate than punishment. There can be little more frustrating than being reproached for something you didn't even know you were doing wrong. On the other hand, anyone acting recklessly needs to be firmly made aware of the consequences of his actions. However, these sorts of mistakes too can generally be avoided in future by training and practice. Highlighting dangers and getting rid of bad habits can work wonders here.

A Place for Punishment

Training may be appropriate in cases of negligence, but depending on the severity of the case, disciplinary action may be unavoidable. I was, for example, extremely pleased to hear that the ATCs at Frankfurt Airport who very nearly caused a crash one night in July 2009, thanks to their casual disregard of regulations, were immediately suspended from duty. Three of four controllers on duty in the tower had left their workplace without permission. A Cessna erroneously started down a runway and missed a waiting Boeing by a hair. The incident went completely unnoticed at first, excepting the Cessna's pilot, naturally. He had been able to lift his machine clear at literally the last second.

Diversionary Tactics and the Blame Game

That means there are, indeed, extreme situations where the first question asked should be "Who's to blame?" The majority of the time, however, it is more productive to ask these questions: "How did this mistake happen?" and "How can it be avoided in future?" Find the causes, not the scapegoats! In many companies, far too much time is spent (almost eagerly) picking over mistakes. This is hardly surprising when you consider that those pinning the blame on others excuse themselves at the same time; they distract attention from their own failings and can reckon on gaining a short-term strategic advantage. I'm guessing that you know the sort: the co-worker who smiles innocently during a meeting and asks: "Oh, wasn't that back when your project turned out to be a flop?" That kind will never miss an opportunity in future to remind you of your failings—particularly when a manager is within earshot. Or think of the line manager who simply won't get a grip on herself: "Jesus, Smith, how could you let that happen? I really expected better from you! And you're usually always so reliable. And now this . . ." She gets so agitated, she forgets to ask the simplest and most important question: "How do we make sure this doesn't happen again?"

Accusations of guilt serve no useful purpose. In fact, this attitude leads directly to the formation of a cover-up mentality. In the medium term, the blame culture that develops leads to everyone suffering as mistakes increase in number, embarrassments are placed center stage, and petty recrimination replaces productive work.

ANTI-CRASH FORMULA

Dealing with mistakes constructively means finding the causes of problems and fixing them—not playing the blame game.

A Mistake Is Rarely a One-Off

Mistakes Multiply: A String of Errors

People make mistakes. They always have and always will. That can be a disquieting thought, particularly regarding safety-critical industries. There is one thing that makes this harsh fact easier to bear: only on the very rarest occasions does a single, fateful mistake lead directly to catastrophe. The infamous big red button—accidentally pressed, setting off the gigantic explosion—exists only in Hollywood fantasy. The majority of cases involve a whole series of errors. One textbook aviation example is the January 1982 crash of an Air Florida Boeing 737 near Washington, DC, whose causes can be traced back to the typical mix of "unfortunate circumstances" and human error.

Mistakes and Bad Luck

It was a freezing day along the eastern seaboard, and it had snowed heavily. Shortly after the Boeing landed, the airport was closed [unfortunate circumstance #1]. Coming from Florida, you aren't going to have the most expansive experience with ice and snow [unfortunate circumstance #2]. Before taking off again, the captain requested de-icing at 14:30. However, maintenance personnel failed to cover inlets on the wings and engines *[mistake #1]*, and ice started forming. Around 30 minutes later, as the plane was supposed to be ready to take off, the tow motor that was supposed to position the aircraft on the runway was unable to gain any traction due to a slippery mixture of ice, snow, and glycol *[unfortunate circumstance #3]*. The captain then made the decision, in open defiance of protocol, to use reverse thrust to move the plane *[mistake #2]*. Indeed, the maneuver failed, but the snow it blew into the air settled onto the aircraft's fuselage *[unfortunate circumstance #4]*. Meanwhile, a queue had formed on the taxi line, and it continued to snow heavily *[unfortunate circumstances #5+6]*. This rendered the previous attempt at deicing "practically worthless."[119] The crew forgot to activate the plane's own anti-icing system *[mistake #3]*. Instead, they attempted to de-ice by maneuvering behind the plane ahead of them and using the heat from its engine exhaust *[mistake #4]*. This was only partially successful and, in fact, may have led to *more* ice forming on the engines. Their 737 was also susceptible to even small amounts of ice on its wings *[unfortunate circumstance #7]*. After waiting for more than an hour, they finally received permission to take off at 15:58.

Dialogue in the Cockpit

The co-pilot was clearly starting to have his doubts. For example, as the captain started the takeoff procedure, he remarked: "God, look at that thing. That doesn't seem right, does it? Uh, that's not right," pointing to his instruments. The captain batted his concerns away: "Yes, it is." But the copilot insisted, at first, "Naw, I don't think that's right." Then immediately gave way: "Ah, maybe it is." Remember, they weren't debating what they were going to have for lunch; this was about a jet airliner with 79 people on board, which was currently accelerating to 150 miles per hour. *[Unfortunate circumstance #8: captain flying with a weak-willed co-pilot]*. Fifty seconds later, the pair were in agreement. "Larry, we're going down," said the co-pilot. His captain answered, "I know." The 737 couldn't accelerate to the required speed. It reached a height of only about 350 feet before losing altitude, clipping a busy road bridge over the Potomac—hitting several vehicles—and crashing into the river. Five passengers and one stewardess survived the crash; one other passenger drowned in the ice-cold river, as rescue attempts were delayed by the resulting traffic chaos.

---

119 Waterkeyn, 124. (Page 123 gives a thorough accident report that is summarized here.)

Chernobyl and Seveso: Similarities

Catastrophes are often characterized by a similar chain of active as well as passive mistakes and unfortunate coincidences. With Chernobyl, for example, "botched construction, inadequate safety precautions, pressure to succeed, and misplaced arrogance" were responsible for causing the most disastrous accident possible in a nuclear power plant. Safety procedures were ignored. The emergency shutdown system was deactivated. Those present included an engineer who "obviously had little understanding of reactor physics."[120] Or think of the aforementioned dioxin release at Seveso ten years before: a chemical plant that was known to be run down. An inexperienced technician mistakenly switched off the stirrer in a reactor vessel, leading it to overheat, and a safety valve failed—all on the weekend, with only a skeleton staff present, so it took an hour before the problem was even noticed.

Example: Karstadt-Quelle

The more complex a system is, the greater the risk of mistakes being made. OK, errors can occur, and the system will keep on functioning. The only problem is that you never know where you are in the error chain. The next lapse, the next accident, any additional mistake, could be the one that breaks the camel's back. Take this "business crash" as an example: the insolvency of the German Karstadt-Quelle retail chain in 2009. Here, too, a whole series of mistakes and misfortunes piled on top of each other until the strain was too much.

Mistakes and Misfortune: The Karstadt-Quelle List

- The company was inherited by a woman with a limited feel for business, who entrusted the company to managers brought in from other industries.
- Power struggles in management that prevented common sense action being taken (for example, rehousing branches of Quelle in Karstadt department stores or exploiting the synergies between the two subsidiaries, Quelle and Neckermann).
- Constant personnel changes at the executive level.

---

120 "Die Katastrophe von Tschernobyl began als Experiment," *Die Welt*, April 3, 1996, www.welt.de.

- A telegenic CEO from the media industry continued claiming the company was doing well—long after it began its accelerating decline towards bankruptcy.

- Attempting to manage a retailer in the same way as an investment bank, making boosting the share price the only priority.

- Selling off the retail estate, only to lease it back at eye-watering prices.

- Being caught napping by new technologies such as the Internet.

- Changing consumer habits, which were making life more difficult for department stores in general.

- The worldwide financial crisis.

- And finally, a strong competitor like the rival Metro Group, which torpedoed a potential state rescue package by proposing the takeover of the group's remaining profitable branches.

Size Doesn't Matter

That was enough to finish off a decades-long presence on main street in Germany. At some point, the loans would be called in.[121] The same goes for the small businessman who starts up that little shop around the corner, the one who somehow misses the well-established competitor two blocks down the road, who doesn't tailor his range of goods to local tastes and, worse, is slack in maintaining hygiene standards. It's not long before he starts to earn a bad reputation, and, to top it all off, he hires an unfriendly salesman, or a clueless Saturday helper, and drives off the few remaining customers.

ANTI-CRASH FORMULA

Not taking individual mistakes seriously is a dangerous game; you never know where you are in the error chain. Always keep that in mind, and act on it.

DEALING WITH MISTAKES AT WORK PROFESSIONALLY

Austrian economist Christian Scholz responded to a journalist who asked how you ruin a business with: "The problem is also there in the business world, that it's

---

121 "Acandor: Wie Missmanagement KarstadtQuelle ruinierte" (Acandor: How Mismanagement ruined KarstadtQuelle), *Wirtschaftswoche*, June 8, 2009, www.wiwo.de.

practically impossible to talk openly about mistakes made by managers."[122] Before mistakes made at work can be approached in a professional manner, the conspiracy of silence has to be broken.

Set an Example

Dealing with Your Own Mistakes

A no-blame culture will be a new direction for most companies. A change of this magnitude can't just be imposed from the top down; rather, a genuine example has to be set. So if you make a mistake, don't hesitate to admit it. Many managers fear appearing to betray uncertainty and a lack of confidence if they do, but in reality, the opposite is the case; someone who can face up to his own mistakes usually wins respect. On the other hand, a denial of something that, in any case, is public knowledge is seen as a sign of weakness. Even worse is attempting to pass the buck for you own bad decisions onto others.

Blame Culture Everywhere

It can be seen both on a large scale and in the details. A while ago, I learned that a school had leased a photocopier. Nothing unusual in that. What was unusual was the length of the contract (14 years) and the expensive leasing rate. You could work out on the back of a placemat that, over the course of the contract, the school was paying for a whole copy shop. Even so, the deal was stoutly defended. The majority of the teaching body were quite serious in their efforts to justify the "investment." This kind of performance can, sadly, be observed again and again during takeover proceedings. Everyone in the business wants to turn back the clock. As the merger is being fully implemented at the latest, even the diehard supporters realize that the hoped-for synergy effects and benefits are never going to make up for the effort and expenditure sunk into the deal. But no one will admit it, nor will anyone learn from it.

Making a Start

It seems that on certain top floors, the idea that there could be another way *has* made the rounds: "In the year just gone, we learned that we should even celebrate failures—if in a different way to successes. Detours broaden your horizons,"

---

122 Matthias Hannemann, "Aus Erfahrung gut. Wie ruiniert man ein Unternehmen?" (Good from Experience: How to Ruin a Company"), *Brand eins*, no. 8 (2007): 74.

claimed, for example, the then Tchibo CEO Dieter Ammer in *Manager Magazin* in 2005.[123] Unfortunately, he didn't specify *how* exactly they celebrated and whether or not his own mistakes were included in the festivities. Daimler chairman Dieter Zetsche also stated in an interview after the breakup of Daimler-Chrysler: "Responsible managers must be allowed to make mistakes. If they aren't prepared to take risks, they leave the company treading water." Without pausing to catch breath, he instantly switched back into justification mode in response to a question about the failure of the merger: "We aren't the only company to reevaluate its strategy in terms of a ten-year plan. It may be the case that not every decision taken will have made sense to an outsider."[124] What is "made sense" supposed to mean here? The attempt to create a globe-spanning automobile empire had been a massively expensive failure for Daimler, destroying billions in value. You could read the gory details every time you opened a newspaper. Yet openly stating this simple fact seemed incredibly difficult.

To the Point

"I got it wrong." "I made a mistake." "That was the wrong decision." "The buck stops here." These are simple phrases. Yet most people would rather bite off their tongue than let these four or five words pass their lips. *You* should break the ice. And don't ruin the effect by tacking on the usual attempts at justification ("Although, at the time, it really couldn't have been foreseen that . . .").

ANTI-CRASH FORMULA

Mistakes must be robbed of their power if you want your staff to be open about them. That means owning your mistakes—especially if you are a manager.

That doesn't mean you should be seizing every opportunity that presents itself to launch into a gushing apology; neither do you need to publicly confess to every little thing that goes wrong. All you need to do is set the right signals at the right time.

---

123 "Zitate, Aperçus und goldene Worte," *Manager Magazin*, January 21, 2005, www.manager-magazin.de/magazin/artikel/0,2828,337509,00.html.

124 "Ich nehme mich selbst nicht so wichtig" (I Don't Take Myself so Important), *Stern*, October 4, 2007, www.stern.de.

Early Warning System for Whistleblowers

That includes treating employees who lift the lid on problems and mistakes fairly. All too often, so-called "whistleblowers" are singled out, put under pressure, harassed. They lose their jobs or resign "voluntarily." Prominent examples include the Dutch EU civil servant Paul van Buitenen, who uncovered corruption and mismanagement in the EU Commission, causing his resignation in 1999, and the Swiss security guard Christoph Meili. In 1997, Meili prevented documents relating to Holocaust victims from being shredded by UBS. The consequences: van Buitenen found his career torpedoed; Meilie was even compelled to emigrate to the United States to escape further harassment. *Harvard Business Manager*, bearing such cases in mind, advises companies to set up an external contact point, where employees will be able to leave tips anonymously. An early warning system could help you to "recognize and deal with misconduct before the damage spreads—even to the extent of forcing bankruptcy."[125] Of course, you might learn some unpleasant truths this way. However, cover-ups and whitewashes aren't going to help—on the contrary. Whistleblowers being forced to go public, after their warnings have fallen on deaf ears internally, demonstrate a disastrous error culture within a business. And that they are then made to suffer for the warnings they make is blame culture in its extreme form.

Don't Punish the Mistake; Punish the Cover-Up

Toyota Production System: Duty of Openness

The deeply rooted shame we feel when admitting a mistake is hard to overcome, positive role models or no. The Japanese can teach us some valuable lessons in promoting a positive error culture. In the Toyota Production System, you face disciplinary action not for *making*, but for *concealing* a mistake. The effect is as simple as it is effective. Imposing sanctions on the concealment of failure creates a new cost-benefit paradigm: I'm better off reporting a mistake. If I don't, I risk being "punished"—if only in the form of facing embarrassing questioning. If, on the other hand, reporting a mistake means facing action against you, as is the norm, that calculation looks quite different: If I say nothing, then there's still the chance

---

125 Cornelia Geißler, "What Is a Whistleblower?" *Harvard Business Manager*, January 2006, 13.

that no one will ever find out about the mistake, and I'll get away with it. In which case, I've got nothing to lose if I keep my mouth shut.

Given this reality, change management expert Winfried Berner recommends a change in attitude regarding mistakes that is as simple as it is effective. Managers should learn to stop asking "How could that happen?" when something goes wrong, and replace it with "How long have you known?"[126] Stick to it, and you will soon see problems being identified sooner, before they have a chance to escalate and get out of hand.

ANTI-CRASH FORMULA

Don't punish the mistake; punish the cover-up! Not "How could that happen?!" but "How long have you known?"

Introduce Routine Analysis of Mistakes

The Ideal Conditions for a No-Blame Culture

In ideal circumstances, it will be normal for employees to talk frankly about mistakes, helping to prevent them recurring in future. This ideal can be brought closer to reality the more employees identify with the company and its successes. Someone who doesn't care about either is unlikely to see good reason to maneuver themselves into an unpleasant situation by highlighting slip-ups and neglect. Or, to put it another way, the more motivated workers are and the more personal responsibility they are prepared to take on, then the more likely they are to pull together in a program to deal with mistakes constructively. Journalist Carsten Jasner touched on this topic in his writing about safety: "In hospitals, the wards where the staff are encouraged to talk openly about mistakes are considered particularly efficient. A rigid hierarchy seems to have equally as fatal consequences as a belief in routine and automation."[127] If you rob workers of their voice, you can hardly expect them to suddenly start speaking out when it comes to mistakes.

---

126 Winfried Berner, "Fehlerkultur: Die Suche nach einem besseren Umgang mit der menschlichen Unvollkommenheit" (Culture of Mistakes: The Search for a Better Handling of Human Imperfection), www.umsetzungsberatung.de.
127 Carsten Jasner, "Gefühlte Sicherheit" (Perceived Safety), *Brand eins,* no. 7 (2009): 52.

Creating the Right Framework

The secret to good personnel management and business management is also to be found in creating an effective framework for the discussion of errors. It doesn't have to be a formal procedure. Wolf Lotter told the story of a small business in Berlin with a staff of 16 employed, tackling damp in homes and offices. On Fridays, the team would relax over a few beers and frankfurters and talk over the workweek. This is a scene reminiscent of the "Communities of Practice" that Xerox instituted after the company realized that the most effective form of CPD for their service engineers wasn't courses and textbooks; it was taking breaks together. The old hands would tell their "war stories" from the copier front line, and their wealth of experience helped everyone involved make smarter choices in future.[128]

Making talking about mistakes normal, making it routine: that is the challenge. The Friday afternoon beer for the blue-collar workers could just as easily be a fixed, weekly time set aside to go over "mistake prevention" for office workers. Indeed, a great deal might be won by avoiding words like "mistake" and "failure"—and their negative connotations—altogether and focusing everyone's attention on how best to plan for the future. A simple list of questions can help to keep the discussion on an objective level.

Useful Questions
- What is the issue at hand? What happened?
- What were the causes?
- What practical steps can we take based on what happened?
- Whose job is it to make them happen?

ANTI-CRASH FORMULA

Ensure that dealing with mistakes becomes a matter of routine. Develop a procedure that suits your company's culture and fits in to your working day.

If you never seem to have to deal with mistakes of any sort at work, start getting suspicious. "The more complex the system, the more often Friday afternoon comes

---

128 Lotter. More about the Xerox communities on the Internet at http://elerning-reviews.com/seufert/docs/xeroxcase-weitergabe-implizites-wissen.pdf.

around," said Wolf Lotter, alluding to the notoriously unreliable cars believed to have been assembled at the end of the week.[129] In all probability, up till now, that wrench in the works is the very last thing you will have gotten to hear about.

HIDING MISTAKES—AND WHAT YOU CAN DO

To conclude, here once more are all the steps you can take to prevent the concealment of mistakes.

ANTI-CRASH FORMULAS AT A GLANCE

1. Dealing with mistakes positively (a no-blame culture) requires a corporate culture that is open, fair, and based on mutual respect; a no-blame culture is one that accepts mistakes are a normal part of the working day.
2. Whether or not mistakes can genuinely be treated as "learning opportunities" depends to a great extent on the way managers deal with their own mistakes.
3. Dealing with mistakes constructively means finding the causes of problems and fixing them—not playing the blame game.
4. Not taking individual mistakes seriously is a dangerous game; you never know where you are in the error chain. Always keep that in mind, and act on it.
5. Mistakes must be robbed of their power if you want your staff to be open about them. That means owning your mistakes—especially if you are a manager.
6. Don't punish the mistake; punish the cover-up! Not "How could that happen?!" but "How long have you known?"
7. Ensure that dealing with mistakes becomes a matter of routine. Develop a procedure that suits your company's culture and fits in to your working day.

---

129 Lotter, 49.

CHAPTER 7

CRASH COMMUNICATION

(Or When Killer Phrases Set the Tone)

+ + + 1980s + + + A McDonnell Douglas comes in to land and overshoots the runway. + + + Everyone on board is killed. + + +

Takeoff and landing are the most dangerous phases of any flight, the time when around 70 percent of all accidents occur. Seasoned fliers might permit themselves a wry smile when less hardy passengers start applauding upon touchdown, but given the facts, you can hardly blame them for expressing their relief. Those with hundreds of landings behind them tend to forget the danger—sometimes including those in the cockpit, with deadly consequences. The co-pilot of an MD-82 is the "pilot flying." About two minutes before landing, he warns the captain: "We're too high and too fast." The captain's response: "We can handle it." A minute later, the same again: "We're too high and too fast." Twenty seconds before touchdown, the co-pilot again attempts to say something. As he does so, the flight engineer nudges the captain, saying: "What's the difference between ducks and co-pilots? Ducks can fly." Thirty seconds later, all three were dead. They had been flying too high and too fast. The aircraft was unable to stop on the runway. All the passengers died with them, as the crash caused the aircraft to burst into flames.

A CAUTIONARY TALE

Flying instructors are very keen on telling this story if they start getting the impression that their pupils are growing complacent and, therefore, liable to underestimate dangers. And particularly so if talk turns rather too euphorically to one's personal heroics and rather too disparagingly to the supposed timidity of other pilots over a drink or two in the pilots' bar. It is a matter of record that aircraft overshoot the runway with some regularity, often causing fires that have devastating consequences for the occupants.[130] Yet from my perspective, this vignette also illustrates another very important point: ignoring colleagues can be very dangerous. And that applies not just in the air, but on the ground too.

Typical Killer Phrases

"We'll manage," is a platitude, an argument used to quell any further dissent. You will probably be familiar with many such phrases from your workplace: "We've always done it this way." (Or alternatively, "We've never done it this way.") "That costs too much." "That won't do any good." "We don't do it that way." "You're not in a position to judge." Full stop. Period. Or maybe you have heard "What worked for 75 years can work for the next 50 years." Those were the words of Alfred Kreidler, head of the eponymous Stuttgart moped and motorbike producer. He was responding to works council representatives who were begging him to replace obsolescent, prewar machinery. The Kreidler patriarch preferred

---

130 "Flugzeugunglücke: Start und Landung sind am gefährlichsten" (Airline Accidents: Takeoff and Landing Are the Most Dangerous), *Focus*, August 20, 2008, www.focus.de.

expensive repairs instead. It wasn't long before the once highly successful firm had to file for bankruptcy.[131]

Communication Is Vital

Communications science has produced the term "killer phrases" to describe unfair language used to squash factual discussions. Killer phrases are just one example of destructive communication (though a very important one). Anyone who has spent any time at all dealing with air accidents and corporate bankruptcies will soon have realized the decisive impact that breakdowns in communication have. Changing markets and buying habits, a fragmented product offering, lack of oversight, aggressive low-cost competition—all these can put a company in danger. But they can only cause a crash if the challenge they pose is not adequately met. It is here that the communication habits within a business play a key role, and breakdowns in communication in the cockpit are of equal import.

CRASH EXAMPLE: DAWSON, TEXAS, MAY 1968

Misfortune—And Mistakes

Again and again, accidents happen that were so avoidable and whose causes were so banal, industry insiders are left speechless. One such incident was the crash of a Braniff Airways Lockheed Electra domestic flight from Houston to Memphis in May 1968. At the time, Braniff was one of the biggest and most well-respected airlines in America. The crash killed 80 passengers in addition to the crew. May 3 saw severe thunderstorms. Meteorologists on the ground had already warned the crew of the extreme weather front ahead before takeoff. In this respect, that typical sequence of unlucky "circumstances" raised its head again. Yet all the other planes crossing the airspace of the southern United States that afternoon (and they were many) reached their destinations in perfect safety. What was different about Braniff flight 352? Against the advice of air traffic control, and in contrast to all (!) the other pilots that day, the captain had decided to fly through the storm front (to find a "gap"). While everything else in the air headed east to divert around the "monster storm," accepting that they needed to take an indirect route to Dallas, the Electra headed west, hoping to slip through the raging storm.

131 "Unternehmer: Nichts ohne mich" (Managers: No Decision Without Me), *Der Spiegel*, no. 11 (1981): 102, here 103.

The cockpit voice recorder preserved the conversation in the cockpit during the doomed flight's final minutes.

Dialogue in the Cockpit

CAPTAIN: "It looks like there's a hole up ahead to me."

CO-PILOT: "Yeah . . ."

At 16:41, the captain requested that passengers stop smoking and buckle their seatbelts, in case "it's a little choppy in the area." Slowly, it started getting bumpy.

At 16:46, the ATC in Dallas, who had expressly warned them about the storm and suggested in vain that they deviate to the east, asked: "Three fifty-two, do you indicate the area you're going into there now as being . . . fairly clear, or do you see openings through it?"

CO-PILOT: "It's not clear . . . but we think we see an opening through it . . . Do you have any reports of hail in this area?" [Hail is extremely dangerous, yet invisible to weather radar.]

ATC: "No, you're the closest one that's ever come to it yet . . . I haven't been able to, anybody to, well, I haven't tried really to get anybody to go through it; they've all deviated around to the east."

CAPTAIN (*cutting off the co-pilot as he tries to answer*): "No, don't talk to him too much. I'm hearing his conversation on this. He's trying to get us to admit we made a big mistake coming through here."

CO-PILOT: "It looks worse to me over there."

The End

Meanwhile, the turbulence continued to worsen. The captain, a 46-year-old veteran with 17 years of flying experience, pressed on undeterred.[132] In the middle of the thunderstorm, it suddenly goes dark. At 16:47, the landing gear warning horn started going off, due to violent strikes to the aircraft that had started affecting the electronics. Finally, in the heart of the storm, the pilot decided to turn back. As the plane made a 180 degree turn, it was caught up in turbulence at 16:47:30 and flipped on its back. Following some hectic maneuvers, the aircraft broke apart at 16:47:42.

---

132 Richter and Wolf, 30. The voice recorder transcripts also come from this volume.

Total Failure of Communication

The official accident investigation by the National Transportation Safety Board concluded that there had been no problems with the communications systems, and radio contact had been maintained until the last moment.[133] True, the technical side of their communications had worked perfectly. And yet this is a case of communication failure, above all, by a captain who stubbornly batted every warning aside and by a co-pilot who wasn't able to assert himself against his boss. A storm of biblical proportions was raging outside, and someone "thinks" that they see an opening? Dozens of human lives are at stake, and raising the threat of hail is simply cut off with a remark like "Don't talk so much; he just wants us to admit we screwed up." The co-pilot is worried they could be making a—potentially fatal—mistake, but he can't bring himself to say anything forceful to his superior. ("Looks worse to me"?) This response is hardly any less absurd than the duck joke we heard in the first example.

CRASH WARNING

If communications break down, soon, everything will break down. Think about *your* company: Are employees' voices heard? Are their suggestions taken seriously?

COMPANY EXAMPLE: GRUNDIG— DOWNFALL OF A HOUSEHOLD NAME

Max Grundig: The Patriarch

"What exactly are you responsible for? Your own home, maybe, but not the business; that belongs to me."[134] Part of a lecture Max Grundig is said to have given his board in the early 80s—at a time when the company's revenues were dramatically collapsing due to competition from the Far East. The Grundig name is synonymous with success, starting in 1945 with the Heinzelmann kit radio. In 1951, Grundig started producing TVs as well. The company grew rapidly, and it

---

133 National Transportation Safety Board, Aircraft Accident Report, June 19, 1969, 13, http://libraryonline.erau.edu/online-fulltext/ntsb/aircraft-accident-reports/AAR69-03.pdf.

134 "Unternehmer: Nichts ohne mich" (Managers: No Decision without Me), *Der Spiegel*, no. 11 (1981): 104.

was soon Europe's biggest radio manufacturer. By the end of the 1970s, Grundig employed almost 40,000 people in 30 factories. Then the rot set in. Cheap Japanese products flooded the market—a threat that Max Grundig simply dismissed as "a myth" at first. After all, his factories were "first class," and according to him, "many Japanese businesses [were] back bedroom outfits."[135]

End of an Era

The founder continued to run the firm with an iron fist, even after it listed on the stock market in 1972. He transferred the majority of shares to a specially created vehicle, the Max-Grundig-Stiftung (Max Grundig Foundation). President of this foundation: one Max Grundig. Chairman of the board of the new publicly listed company: one Max Grundig.[136] What followed is not long in the telling. Continuing economic difficulties forced Grundig into the arms of Holland's Philips in the early 1980s, with Philips increasing its share of the firm in 1984 and forcing Max Grundig to step down. In 1998, Philips sold up to a Bavarian consortium, but losses continued, and Grundig was forced to file for bankruptcy in 2003, with its banks refusing to extend its credit. The company was broken up, much of it being taken over by a Turkish holding company; Grundig-branded flat-screen TVs are still being produced in Turkey. At one point, more than 20,000 people in Nuremberg worked for Grundig. Now, a few hundred take care of sales and marketing.[137]

The Consequences of Destructive Communication

Of course, many factors will have contributed to the downfall of this once prestigious brand, including cheap competition from the Far East, against which too little was done, too late (with, for example, the production of a whole series of different video systems that couldn't compete against the already established VHS standard). Yet if press reports about the company founder can be taken at face value, then his autocratic communication style was at least partially responsible for the way the company headed unstoppably towards bankruptcy, with all the maneuverability

---

135 "Unternehmen: Heinzelmann gegen Postillion" (Business: Heinzelmann against Postillion), *Der Spiegel*, no. 17 (2003): 126.
136 "Max Grundig," Who's Who, www.whoswho.de.
137 "Insolvenz: Grundig" (Insolvencies: Grundig), *Der Spiegel*, June 19, 2009, www.spiegel.de.

of an oil tanker. How many ideas, how much passion can you expect from your board if you tell them to their faces that they might run their own homes, but not the company? Anyone working in an atmosphere like that would have needed to be brave indeed to point out any problems and make any suggestions for change. And how much constructive criticism would a manager be able to expect, even if he was clearly steering the company into difficulties? When full and frank discussion is made impossible, when objections and concerns are shot down, when new ideas are squashed and employees are forbidden from having an opinion, the situation becomes critical.

"DESTRUCTIVE COMMUNICATION": THE CRASH BEGINS WITH THE SAID (AND UNSAID)

Tenerife: A Textbook Example of Destructive Communication

What do I mean by "destructive communication"? To answer this question, we shall make a brief layover at the beginning of the book: the devastating 1977 Tenerife crash, when two 747s collided on the fog-shrouded runway of Los Rodeos Airport and almost 600 people lost their lives. Doubtless, the circumstances were unusually difficult—the small Canary Islands airport was packed to bursting, visibility almost non-existent. On the other hand, the crews of both planes knew that their counterparts were waiting in the immediate vicinity for permission to take off, experienced pilots were sitting in the cockpits, and the communications equipment was in perfect working order. The accident didn't happen because of mechanical failure or because it was foggy, but because there was a breakdown in communication between the parties involved. Let's revisit the questions I asked at the beginning of the book:

1. What would have happened if the co-pilot of the KLM aircraft had contradicted the pilot flying? ("I consider that too dangerous.")
2. What would have happened if the cockpit crew of the Pan Am plane had raised the alarm with air traffic control? ("We're still on the runway.")
3. What would have happened if the KLM captain had asked the Spanish air traffic control to repeat the decisive order, just to be sure? ("That means we have clearance for takeoff?")

4. What would have happened if the KLM captain had inquired, to be on the safe side, if the runway was clear? ("Has Pan Am 1736 already left the runway?")

5. What would have happened if the pilot of the KLM plane had stated, audible for everyone, "KLM—beginning takeoff"?

Obstacles

None of these possibilities came about, presumably because those involved felt one or more of the following:

- They were afraid of contracting authority (1).
- They wanted to save face by avoiding admitting to doubts and uncertainty (2 and 4).
- They preferred hearing what they wanted to hear over asking awkward questions (3).
- They considered clearly informing others of what they were doing a waste of time (5).

Forms of Destructive Communication

Hand on heart: how often does your business day take a similar course to this? I am willing to bet that you need only think back to the last departmental meeting for two or three similar examples to come to mind. In my understanding, "destructive" communication is characterized by behavior such as the following: excessive reticence; failure to express reservations or personal opinions; opportunism; making vague innuendoes and hasty assumptions; withholding information; worse, making threats or attempting to intimidate, coupled with insinuations and personal attacks. "Constructive" communication, in contrast, consists—in my opinion—of open, respectful, and solution-orientated collaboration, though this is an ideal that is often far from reality. Most of the time, there aren't even any ill intentions behind crash communication (for example, trying to "get one over" a rival). The quotidian reality is one of habit and simple lack of understanding of the issue. After all, everyone can speak, can't he?

How Communication Works (or Not):
The Container Model of Communication

As long as we don't happen to be abroad, or in the middle of a marital dispute, day-to-day communication is normally a simple business; we wrap what we want up in speech and assume that our interlocutors will simply understand what we "mean." This kind of "common sense" corresponds to an extremely simplified model of communication: the transmitter (T) encodes a message (M) into words, from which the receiver (R) decodes the message. If both use the same "code" and transmit and receive on the same channel, nothing can go wrong.

$$\text{Transmitter (T)} \rightarrow \text{Message (M)} \rightarrow \text{Receiver (R)}$$

In linguistics, this concept is known as the "container model" of communication. Academia has long since moved on from this naïve oversimplification, for communication is in reality much more complex. Which factors play a part?

Diversity of Meaning: The "Four-Ears" Model

The container model presupposes a completely unambiguous message, whose meaning is crystal clear. Language is, however, rather more complex than that. Take an average, ordinary family. Do you really believe that each family member defines the concepts "order, punctuality, hard work" the same way, or even "peace and quiet"? Each individual word is open to a different interpretation (and indeed often will be interpreted differently). Now, we take these words, ambiguous to start off with, and we make whole sentences out of them. It can hardly be much of a surprise if these sentences themselves are open to quite different interpretations.

Hamburg psychologist Friedemann Schulz von Thun brilliantly explained the concept with his "four ears" or four sides model. According to this, each communication contains both *factual information* and an *appeal* to the receiver; it also reveals something about the sender (*self-revelation*) and defines the *relationship* of the interlocutors.

Examples of the Ambiguity of Language

In communication seminars, this model is often illustrated using the example of the (male) backseat driver, who says: "It's green." (Factual information: "The traffic light is green"; possible appeal: "Put your foot on it!"; self-revelation: "I'm in a hurry" or "I'm a better driver than you"; statement about the relationship: "I'll tell you how you drive, missy!") How is the (female) driver likely to react? This stereotypical seminar example has reached the stage where it can almost blind us to how universal this effect is. When, for example, the co-pilot on that Braniff Elektra stared into the storm and said nervously, "It looks worse to me over there," then, along with the factual statement about possible risk, was an appeal ("Wouldn't it be better to turn around?"), a self-revelation (concern), and an indication of their relationship ("I'm just making a suggestion, but, of course, the final decision as captain is yours").

The Receiver's Interpretation

At the same time, the magnitude of the room for interpretation is revealed by what is actually a simple sentence: the captain can either pick up on these additional messages, unwittingly miss them in the stress of the situation, or consciously ignore them. The receiver decides whether or not to turn a "blind ear." Unfortunately, this decision is often made subconsciously. Three out of four messages are blocked out. Do you turn a "blind ear" sometimes? (Pro tip: if you do, it will likely be the ear you use for "factual information.") Do you listen differently when you are under pressure? Do you listen differently to different people?

Complex Means of Communication: The 55-38-7 Rule

Just as beloved and oft-cited as the four-sides model is a study by the American psychologist Albert Mehrabian, which found that only 7 percent of a message is communicated verbally (i.e., by the words themselves), with 38 percent being communicated by tone of voice and 55 percent nonverbally (through gestures, facial expression, and body language).[138] When mention is made of this "55-38-7 Rule," it is often forgotten that Mehrabian was specifically researching presentations to an audience. Nevertheless, we all know that nonverbal communication can completely reverse the meaning of a verbal statement: in irony, for example. With the right (or wrong) intonation, the sentence, "You really outdid yourself on this project!"

---

138 Mehrabian, Albert and Susan R. Ferris, "Inference of Attitudes from Nonverbal Communication in Two Channels," *Journal of Consulting Psychology*, no. 31 (1967): 248.

harbors a devastating criticism. We have many ways of transmitting and receiving meaning, through intonation, volume, vocal quality, facial expression, and body language, all depending on the current situation. If the co-pilot had screamed, "It looks really bad over there!" with hands raised defensively and a shocked expression on his face, the message would have been a different one, and the appeal to turn back may well have gotten through.

ANTI-CRASH FORMULA

Interpersonal communication is everything except unambiguous. Consciously and subconsciously, we use numerous different means to communicate. The downside to this diversity: ambiguity and susceptibility to error.

The Relationship Level Dominates

The Relationship Determines the Content

Just like Schulz von Thun, the linguist and philosopher Paul Watzlawick emphasizes how every communication says something about the relationship between the interlocutors. However, Watzlawick also draws attention to the increased importance of the relationship aspect when uncertainty arises: "Every communication has a content and relationship aspect such that the latter classifies the former."[139] We can see it on any given day when a good argument falls on deaf ears because someone "struck the wrong tone" beforehand. And we take it into account instinctively, by waiting for a "good time" to talk to the boss, for example, or to bring up a tricky subject at home. If everything is running smoothly at the relationship level, then factual information will be transmitted more effectively. If things aren't running smoothly, communication as a whole breaks down.

Fatal Hesitancy

Just how extreme this effect can be was demonstrated by the 1990 Avianca Flight 52 crash described in the first chapter. You may recall that the plane was heading from Medellin to New York; due to bad weather, the New York

---

139 Paul Wtzlawick, Janet H. Beavin, and Don D. Jackson, *Menschliche Kommunikation* (Human Communication), 9th ed. (Bern: Huber, 1996), 56.

ATC repeatedly stacked it in a holding pattern. The first attempt to land failed and had to be aborted. Although they were almost out of fuel, the Columbian co-pilot wasn't able to stand up to the brusque air traffic controller at JFK Airport and make clear the seriousness of the situation. He continued to zealously carry out instructions and contented himself with making vague remarks: "Climb and maintain three thousand, and ah, we're running out of fuel, sir." Since this is perfectly normal for any aircraft shortly before landing, it will have sounded completely mundane for the ATC. At some point, the co-pilot seems to have given up completely, answering the captain's persistent questioning ("What did he say?") with a simple "The guy is angry."[140] The fuel will run out in any second, and the co-pilot lets himself be intimidated by the supposed bad mood of the ATC? And people talk about "businesslike" communication. Even in the face of disaster, people obviously struggle to speak objectively.

ANTI-CRASH FORMULA

If the relationship level is working, then, as a rule, the message itself will get across. If the relationship isn't working—if the atmosphere is dominated by arguments, aversion, or mistrust, for example—then a breakdown in communications is inevitable.

You Have to Want Good Communications

Standardized Terminology in the Cockpit

A wise man once said that the commonest form of human communication was misunderstanding. Interpersonal communication is extremely complex—and hence open to misinterpretation. The airline industry has drawn some radical conclusions from this fact. Communication in the cockpit is now as regimented and standardized as possible. Pilots don't just say what they feel like; instead, a fixed terminology has been developed for anything that might happen. That keeps the uncertainty and room for misinterpretation of "normal" everyday language to a minimum.

---

140 www.tailstrike.com/250190.htm.

Constructive Communication in Business

The working day is too colorful and diverse for the language of business to be as standardized as that of the air, but the importance of clear communication to business success has long been obvious. Year after year, employees attend seminars in their thousands to be inducted into the communication fold.[141] A quickie course in the four-sides model will, however, have little effect if conditions in the business as a whole aren't up to scratch. "Good" communication needs to be the stated and lived aim of the entire company. My understanding of "good" (constructive) communication is an overwhelmingly factually and solutions-oriented model that is driven by openness and fairness. Mutual respect and appreciation, making the effort to understand your interlocutor, are the soil in which constructive communication thrives. If this base is lacking, then you can talk till the cows come home about the factual and relationship levels, but little if anything is going to change.

The Prerequisite: A Positive Company Culture

Good communication is only going to happen if it is made part of a positive company culture. Naturally, this applies to training and consultancy businesses as well. I know more than one team where remarks like "He shouldn't take himself so seriously," or "What does that kid think he's playing at?" are commonplace. This can hardly be construed as an attempt to constructively deal with problems. Do you imagine that these folks share their information as a matter of routine and are offering up creative solutions? Or perhaps you already suspect that the "kid" has long since been looking for another job?

Economic Grounds for Effective Communication

Perhaps "good communication" sounds to you like the wishful thinking of a hand-wringing do-gooder, far removed from the harsh realities of business life. For sure, you might think, be fair, be open, but that's an ideal that you can, at best, make an honest effort to attain. It is surely impossible to achieve in reality. Yet this has nothing to do with producing a cushy, cozy atmosphere. Openly expressed conflict is an important part of a positive business culture. If things are always swept under the carpet, sooner or later, you are going to trip over them. This is why pilots

---

141 On November 18, 2009, the databank accessible at www.seminarmarkt.de produced 3,751 offers for the key word "Kommunikation"—and that is just part of the market.

routinely talk through the flight after landing, in order to resolve any conflicts. Above and beyond that, the "feel-good factor" directly impacts the bottom line. "Managers often underestimate how poor employee morale impacts first upon customers and finally upon results," noted German business daily *Handelsblatt*, in relation to the travails of companies like Karstadt, Ihr Platz, and Dresdner Bank.[142] A study by the Wharton School of Business backs this up with hard figures. Economists surveyed employees of *Fortune's* "100 Best Companies to Work For" on their levels of job satisfaction. The result: on average, the shares of companies with satisfied employees saw double the gains between 1998 and 2005 of those companies with lower levels of employee satisfaction.[143]

It is, of course, obvious that job satisfaction strongly correlates to the way a company treats its workers. Communication is a significant part of this. After all, fair communication is like paying into a "trust account," from which you can make withdrawals in difficult times, during periods of change, or during disputes, for example. Making this kind of "down payment" is essential as suddenly demanding trust in times of crisis is pointless. Imagine just how many Opel workers were still listening to the GM managers who went on a tour through Europe in autumn 2009, after the Magna rescue deal had collapsed.

ANTI-CRASH FORMULA

Good communication is only possible if it is embedded in a positive company culture.

DAILY COMMUNICATION SINS

Reasons for Destructive Communication

What role does destructive communication play in business? And how can you recognize it? Once more, destructive communication is usually used unintentionally.

---

142 Lars Reppesgaard, "Missmanagement: Wie sich Firmen selbst demontieren" (Mismanagement: How Companies Disassemble Themselves), *Handelsblatt*, September 28, 2006, www. handelsblatt.com.

143 Olaf Storbeck, "Satisfied employees are more productive: So Much For Social Odds and Ends," *Handelsblatt*, July 16, 2007, www.handelsblatt.com. (For the Wharton study see also http:// papers.ssrn.com/sol3/papaers.cfm?abstract_id=985735.)

Whether its use is intentional or not, generally speaking, unfair communication serves the following purposes:

- Silence critics
- Block changes and new ideas
- Wriggle out of doing overtime or unpleasant tasks
- Pass the buck
- Push through personal interests
- Avoid admitting personal mistakes
- Let us see how these aims are put into practice.

Killer Phrases

Categories of Killer Phrases

Take some time to familiarize yourself with the following list. Which of these phrases have you encountered before (perhaps even used yourself)? It won't take much guesswork to figure out the motivations behind them.

1. "We've always (never) done it this way."
2. "That's difficult (too time-consuming, expensive, etc.)!"
3. "It didn't work back then either."
4. "We've tried all of that."
5. "Other people have tried that."
6. "That can't be done (here)."
7. "That won't work here (in this company)."
8. "There's no way the boss will agree to that."
9. "It's always worked perfectly well as it is."
10. "We'll never manage that!"
11. "We don't have time for that now."
12. "It can't be done right now."
13. "Without wishing to cut the discussion short . . ."
14. "Let's not be too hasty."
15. "Let's get back to the topic at hand . . ."
16. "It'll work out."

17. "We'll manage."
18. "You have a negative attitude."
19. "Moaning and whining never got anything done."
20. "That's not our job."
21. "That's not our problem."
22. "That's nothing to do with us."
23. "I'm only covering here."
24. "You're hardly in a position to judge."
25. "You don't have the experience" or "You're too young."
26. "If you really want to make a fool of yourself . . ."
27. "And the Earth is flat, lol."
28. "You cannot be serious."
29. "Let's take an objective look at this for a second . . ."
30. "I'd say the same thing in your place."

The Motivation behind Particular Killer Phrases

The list could go on and on. Killer phrases are designed to silence the person they are directed at and to prevent uncomfortable discussions. They are often used to defend the status quo (1–10), to communicate the motto "It can wait" (11–15), to put down objections (16–19), to avoid work (20–23), or to intimidate and/ or unsettle others—implying that their motives or simply their competence leave something to be desired (24–30). Killer phrases always come in the form of generalizations, presented in a condescending, patronizing manner. The substance of what the other person has to say is not taken seriously. Instead, he is simply outmaneuvered from a position of authority as those who lack factual arguments take refuge in the "relationship level."

Company Idiolects

Alongside commonly known platitudes, many companies and departments cultivate their own "dialects" of killer phrases:

- "Our customers don't want that."
- "Our trading partners won't accept it."
- "The price is the only thing that matters anyway."

- "Here at Joe Bloggs Industries, we do it like this . . ."
- "As the market leaders, we . . ."

The Decline and Fall of the Swiss Watch Industry

Killer phrases indicate more than just a lack of respect towards the other person; they are also typical of a culture hostile to innovation. In most cases, it's about preventing change: not in the little things and certainly not in the big things. Many companies (like Grundig and Kreidler) have gone under thanks to this "but we've always done it this way" attitude—as have entire industries. One well-known example is the Swiss watch industry, which shrank into insignificance by the end of the 1970s. The Japanese had conquered the world market with their quartz watches. Ironically, it was the Swiss who had developed this technology in the first place. A group of Swiss manufacturers presented the new wristwatches at the 1970 Basel Watch Fair, but accustomed to success, the industry remained convinced that "real" watches had cogs and gears inside and that nothing needed to change. The result: watch exports halved between 1977 and 1983. The Swiss share of the world market fell from 43 to 15 percent, and of 90,000 who were once employed in the industry, only 40,000 remained.[144]

The Effects of Killer Phrases

Killer phrases reinforce groupthink (cf. the classic "We've always done it this way"), they poison the working atmosphere by putting co-workers down ("Other people have already tried that, you know"), and they make the working day a trial ("That's not my job, mate"). If you do not want that to happen, take firm action against killer phrases.

ANTI-CRASH FORMULA

Don't put up with killer phrases! They are a sign of narrow-mindedness, laziness, and arrogance.

---

144 "Geschichte der Armbanduhren" (The History of Wristwatches), www.uhrenwerkzeug.com, and "333 Millionen Mal Brot für die Uhrenindustrie" (333 Billions Times Bread for the Watches Industry), *Bieler Tagblatt*, May 31, 2006, www.bielertagblatt.ch.

. . . And Other Destructive Forms of Communication

Killer phrases are a powerful indicator that constructive discussion is not taking place within a company, thus increasing the risk of malfunctions and crashes. There are other forms of communication with similarly devastating effects, which are often overlooked.

Silence

Sign of Fear

A silent co-pilot has been found to be responsible, at least in part, for a number of air accidents, as he looked on and did nothing while the captain made critical mistakes (see chapter 2). Silence can also be a sign of uncertainty and fear in the business world. A "culture of silence" lacks the warning voices that are needed to nip problems in the bud. Think of German industrialist Philipp Daniel Merckle, who considered a culture of silence a factor in the way his father Adolf Merckle was able to set up a network of companies of Byzantine complexity and to gamble away a large part of his fortune on the stock market. This form of silence can frequently be found in authoritarian structures and strongly hierarchical company cultures.

Sign of Resistance

Equally, silence can be an indicator of defiance and resistance or, at best, indifference. Anyone who has tried to win over colleagues in a meeting only to be met with a wall of silence after putting his all into a presentation will know what I am talking about. It is like talking to a brick wall: crossed arms, people engrossed in their files or totally concentrated on their Blackberry. There is a total lack of verbal feedback. What they are saying *non-verbally* ranges from "Blah, blah, blah" to "Count me out." There is a backstory to this silence. Cost-cutting measures and the loss of dearly held perks are a factor in many companies, and disillusionment regarding unkept promises and misleading statements by management can also play a role. Silence can by no means always be read as consent. A defiant (or lethargic) silence will identify the around two-thirds of employees revealed to be apathetic and unmotivated every year by the Gallup Engagement Index; it also includes the roughly 12 percent who have already mentally composed their resignation letters.

Interestingly, the Gallup researchers found the principal root of the problem to be a lack of recognition, interest, and communication from the immediate line manager—in short, more silence.[145]

Sign of Power

And finally, there is also that icy silence used by the powerful to crush underlings. In these cases, silence is characteristic of superiority rather than helpless defiance. Rumor has it that VW boss Ferdinand Piëch enjoys using this form of corrosive silence to express his displeasure, even to top-level executives.

ANTI-CRASH FORMULA

Silence where a reaction is called for is a warning signal. Whether it indicates fear, noncompliance, or aggression depends on the position of the silent in the hierarchy.

Agreement, and the Flipside of Agreement

Obviously, all of us are happy when we can secure agreement, so we are unlikely to question it too closely when we get it. What I am talking about here is, however, not carefully considered and well-founded consensus, but the hasty nod to everything one is presented with. In some meetings, the majority of those present start nodding before their boss can even finished his sentence. What he was actually going to say could still have gone in any direction—just agree with everything, that was the main thing. Opportunism, resignation, indifference, careerism, or having no ideas of one's own: all these can be concealed behind unthinking agreement. For the woman or man at the top, this can all be quite agreeable—at first. The drawback is that little can be achieved with a group of yes men.

ANTI-CRASH FORMULA

If agreement comes suspiciously easily, ask yourself what hidden grounds might lie behind such hasty consent.

---

145 http://pdf.berkemeyer.net/Gallup-Studie.pdf.

Moaning and Whining

Those Who Love to Moan

As a pilot, I know that the problem with mist is that it limits visibility. In the same way, the doom and gloom spread by pessimists also limits horizons, keeping companies from taking off as mist does a plane. It might help the person doing the moaning—in the short term at least—to let off some steam, but it does nothing to produce a solution, either for him or for the business. The energy expended complaining could be more productively channeled elsewhere. A culture of complaining is par for the course in German companies, at all levels of the hierarchy: about the unfair boss, about high taxes and low wages, about the food in the canteen, about the weather (too hot, too dry, too cold, too wet), about the impossible targets set by management, about competition from those darned sweatshops in the Far East, about the idiots in product development (or management or sales or logistics), about anything and everything, in fact, ad infinitum.

Dangers of a Complaint Culture

Up to a point, this is, of course, all perfectly natural. However, if complaints become the prevailing topic of conversation in the office and on the shop floor and everything that happens in the company is compulsively picked apart, then you have a real problem on your hands. Constant moaning and groaning, unfortunately, not only is often infectious, but it also deadens initiative, blinds people to opportunities, and absorbs a disproportionate amount of their focus and attention. The kind of problem bellyaching can cause is demonstrated by the case of the two Northwest Airlines pilots who became so involved in a discussion about the airline's employment conditions that they quite simply flew past their destination airport in Minneapolis (chapter 5). That they were singing the company's praises during this slight lapse in concentration can safely be considered unlikely.

ANTI-CRASH FORMULA

Don't let the noise produced by the moaners drown out the voices of those producing solutions or distract you from your targets.

Paying Lip Service, Lies, Threats

Why Cheap Talk Is Anything but Cheap

There are phrases that can provoke only a tired grin: "Our employees are our most valuable resource." "The customer is central to everything we do." "We have a culture of openness and respect." "Outside-the-box thinkers welcome." These are nothing more than vague expressions of intention, often with little grounding in reality. In fact, it is lip service, and only the naïve are likely to buy it. At first glance, you might think these kind of phrases do little harm, but the truth is they fatally undermine trust in a company's culture of communication. How seriously can you take people who have such a slippery grip on reality when it comes down to daily business? The transition from paying lip service to tactical lying is a fluid one ("No, no one is thinking about downsizing." "No, the company is not being sold."). Management often believes that the circumstances offer them no other choice—they are afraid of spooking the workers or of making news public prematurely. In doing so, they frequently underestimate the demotivating effect and the loss of trust that sets in as soon as the cat is out of the bag. Simply coming out with the truth (or admitting that future developments remain uncertain) is often the best course of action.

How Threats Work

And then there are departments that are run like a dictatorship, with threats, intimidation, and humiliation the order of the day. "I'm going to make your life a living hell." "You'll regret that!" "If you don't agree to this, don't bother coming in tomorrow." This kind of language is normally only ever used in one-on-one situations where there is no chance of being observed by others. (There are said to be people who enjoy using the elevator for this.) At the same time, anyone prepared to say in public that "it's time to nail someone to the wall" is hardly going to shy away from using strong language in meetings.

The Devastating Consequences

This type of communication is "crash relevant" because, just like killer phrases, it silences people, prevents objections and constructive criticism from being heard, and blocks change. In an increasingly complex and fast-paced business landscape, the long-term results will be disastrous. Nobody is infallible, and the authoritarian "absolute dictators" of the business world too are bound to slip up sooner or later. The negative consequences of hierarchies stressed past breaking point were, of course, already noted in chapter 2, under the heading "Power Distance."

ANTI-CRASH FORMULA

In the long run, lip service, lies, and threats will fatally undermine any business. Motivation plummets, problems are no longer resolved, and innovation is blocked off.

PROFESSIONAL BUSINESS COMMUNICATION

The Advantages of Fair Communication

There can be no doubt that resolving to set a good example and seeking to personally avoid the use of killer phrases—as well as indifferent silence, opportunism, pointless whining, and even threats—during one's working day is a noble act. Managers should be careful not to underestimate how strongly their personal behavior affects the atmosphere in their department. Besides, those attuned to the niceties of communication have more room to maneuver and can navigate more easily around problem areas. Additionally, there are a couple of practical steps that can be taken to make it easier to discuss matters objectively and with the search for a solution firmly in mind.

Seven Golden Rules for Mutual Understanding

Actually, we are indeed all aware of how difficult it can be to avoid misunderstandings and discord. Nevertheless, most people lose their cool more often than they'd care to admit and say things in the heat of the moment that they later regret. The following thoughts and "rules" might help you to communicate calmly and collectedly.

Everyone Lives in His Own World: "Seeing" Other People

Everyone carries with him his own formative experiences, ways of perceiving the world, life experience, values, and beliefs. You cannot assume that the "world" of the person you are talking to matches your own. What for one person may be an "objective suggestion" might be a slap in the face to another. And what one person "obviously meant to say" might be completely missed by the person he was trying to communicate with, if he is operating from within a different experience horizon.

Everything You Say Can Be Misunderstood: Always Be Aware

Every statement can be misunderstood . . . even an apparently harmless remark about the weather ("Have we really reached the point where we're reduced to small talk?"). Think of the matter-of-factness of the New York air traffic controller that was interpreted as "anger" by the intimated co-pilot of the ill-fated aircraft.

Ninety Percent of Communication Is Nonverbal: Pay Attention to Nonverbal Signals

Your gestures, facial expressions, voice, intonation, personal space, and body language are all sending a message. Suppose a manager concludes a presentation with the remark "Any questions?" This can be anything from intimidation to a friendly invitation, depending on his body language.

One Cannot Not Communicate: You Are Always Communicating!

"One cannot not communicate" is surely the most oft-quoted line from Paul Watzlawick's work: Everything you do communicates something—even when you are doing "nothing." Whether you greet someone or not, speak or keep your counsel, maintain or avoid eye contact, it is impossible to avoid sending out signals.

It's Never Just about "X": "Objectivity" Is a Fairytale

There is a myth of long-standing that work is an objective business. Maintaining status, self-interest, and the fear of losing face always play their part. Hence, there is a massive difference between public and private criticism. That hackneyed phrase "It's nothing against you personally" is an empty one for this very reason.

Emotion Is Stronger than Reason: Emotion Counts Double

Your command of facts and figures might be perfect, but competence is nothing without good working relationships. Employees who are concentrating on salvaging their self-esteem will be able to contribute little of constructive or imaginative value to a discussion. Have you ever thought to yourself, "I'm not working with *him*!"? If not, you have probably never had to deal with stubbornness, tit-for-tat behavior, or with people being messed around with.

Action Always Has a Motivation: Seeing through Others

Even when emotion is not immediately apparent, it can still play a role in communication. Maybe someone is flatly refusing to take your "sensible" proposal on board because he won't be able to sell it to his superiors. Or maybe he is being stubborn because you rejected *his* proposal the last time round. Or he is trying to find ways to shoot you down because he had his mind made up in someone else's favor from the start.

Those who can admit to themselves that these drives inform their own, as well as others', behavior will perhaps be better placed to react in a calm and collected manner when under pressure or if differences of opinion arise—and even outdo themselves in dealing with the situation.

ANTI-CRASH FORMULA

If you truly understand communication, you will be much better placed to handle tricky situations.

Useful Methods for Dealing with Killer Phrases and Groupthink

We all want to be able to hold our head up high. We want to preserve our status, reach our goals, and, quite simply, we want to look good. That often makes it extremely difficult not to dismiss criticism with killer phrases and to remain open to change. Here are a couple of practical tips to help you keep bad habits at bay.

Make Killer Phrases Taboo

Individual Plan

There are many books that can tell you what you as an individual can do to protect yourself from killer phrases: Let them bounce off you with a smile and ignore them. You can point them out for what they are. ("That is a killer phrase and adds nothing to the conversation.") Another possibility is to counter with a follow-up question.

("That won't work." → "Why not exactly?" → "You don't have the experience." → "What, then, do I need to take into consideration, in your opinion?")

Group Plan

If you want to raise the tone of the department as a whole, then you can agree to rules of conduct. For example, every time someone uses a killer phrase, he has to put a dollar in the "killer phrase box." A new "treasurer" is selected for each meeting. Or, the chair of the meeting shows a yellow card. Two yellows are followed by red—change of speaker. If that sounds too silly, try the following: note down your department's favored killer phrases on a flipchart and put it in a prominent position in the meeting room. You will be surprised at how often and how effectively the poster is referred to.

Encourage Original Thought

Get Your Thinking Caps On

If departments and companies themselves wish to be able to develop and grow—and not become stuck with an outdated worldview and working methods—then it is imperative that "dissent" be permitted. One proven method for encouraging new ideas and points of view is putting on one of Edward de Bono's "thinking hats." Speakers embody different roles, depending on which "hat" they happen to be wearing. Black stands for discernment (disadvantages, risks, problems), yellow for optimism (advantages, opportunities), white for strict focus on information (facts, numbers, data), red for vemotions (feelings, intuitions, opinions), green for creativity (new ideas, the provocative, the crazy), and blue stands for order, for the bird's-eye-view perspective that incorporates all the other viewpoints (as moderator, for example, or at the end of the discussion).[146] Obviously, you don't need to get the sewing basket out and make any actual hats; a colored card will do just as well. In earlier times, court jesters quite intentionally wore a different type of hat. Nowadays, when it comes to critical, long-term decisions and strategic thinking, it pays to stray off the beaten track. You can have the entire group change hats together (i.e., discussing first "white," then "red," then the "green" aspects) or have them divide the roles between themselves.

---

146 Edward de Bono, *Six Thinking Hats*, 13th ed. (Boston: Back Bay Books, 1999).

Brainstorming

Brainstorming sessions have a similar purpose; here, too, the objective is being able to express thoughts and ideas openly, without fear of censure and without precipitous judgments being reached. The hat method has the added advantage that allocating clearly defined roles makes existing hierarchical positions less of a factor.

Keep Your Ear to the Ground: Use the Wisdom of Your Employees

See Your Employees' Potential

"Troublemakers" have a bad reputation in the business world. Think of the employee who starts his sentences with, "Yes, but . . ." Many a manager starts thinking something along the lines of "How am I going to crush him?" A tricky balancing act is needed here: where do you draw the line between plain old grumbling and complacency and justified caution? Those in management positions who can divest themselves of the fantasies of power and superiority that many associate with the role (know everything, do everything, always have the last word—packaged in the most polite terms, of course, and with the desired "cooperative" quality) will have won a great battle right at the start. Most branches of business today are far too complex for any single manager to be able to keep on top of all the details. Those who do not and indeed cannot know it all are well advised to respect and make judicious use of their colleagues' combined wisdom. Why else do we employ highly qualified staff?

It Pays to Follow Up on Things

Frontline workers on the shop floor or with direct customer contact are very often the ones who know where the problems lie and what needs to be changed. Very seldom are they listened to. "That won't work here" can be a generalizing killer phrase, but in some cases it can be a justified assessment. It is always worthwhile to ask them, "Why do you think that?" and ask yourself, "And what if it's true?" The same can be said of similar notes of caution, like "That could cause problems." What is stopping you from digging deeper and asking, "What makes you say that?" Indeed, you should be overjoyed if employees are (still) prepared to express their concerns. Who wants to be the bearer of bad news, after all?

Listen

Do you recall the emergency landing made on the Azores by the Air Transat plane, after gliding nearly 75 miles over the Atlantic (chapter 5)? This near disaster was caused by a fuel leak in the Airbus 330's number two engine. It led (together with a miscalculation by the captain) to the aircraft running out of fuel over the ocean. And the cause of the leak itself was an ill-fitting replacement part that had been installed during maintenance work and had damaged a fuel line. The mechanic responsible had notified his superior—but his concerns were dismissed.

ANTI-CRASH FORMULA

Introduce targeted routines and codes of conduct that prevent employee concerns from being ignored or swept under the carpet before being duly considered.

DESTRUCTIVE COMMUNICATION—AND WHAT YOU CAN DO

In conclusion, here are all the anti-crash formulas at a glance.

ANTI-CRASH FORMULAS AT A GLANCE

1. Interpersonal communication is everything except unambiguous. Consciously and subconsciously, we use numerous different means to communicate. The downside to this diversity: ambiguity and susceptibility to error.
2. If the relationship level is working, then, as a rule, the message itself will get across. If the relationship isn't working—if the atmosphere is dominated by arguments, aversion, or mistrust, for example—then a breakdown in communications is inevitable.
3. Good communication is only possible if it is embedded in a positive company culture.
4. Don't put up with killer phrases! They are a sign of narrow-mindedness, laziness, and arrogance.
5. Silence where a reaction is called for is a warning signal. Whether it indicates fear, noncompliance, or aggression depends on the position of the silent in the hierarchy.

6. If agreement comes suspiciously easily, ask yourself what hidden grounds might lie behind such hasty consent.

7. Don't let the noise produced by the moaners drown out the voices of those producing solutions or distract you from your targets.

8. In the long run, lip service, lies, and threats will fatally undermine any business. Motivation plummets, problems are no longer resolved, and innovation is blocked off.

9. If you truly understand communication, you will be much better placed to handle tricky situations.

10. Introduce targeted routines and codes of conduct that prevent employee concerns from being ignored or swept under the carpet before being duly considered.

UTILIZING RESOURCES: COMPANY RESOURCE MANAGEMENT

FLYING: IN SAFE HANDS

"Large airlines are safer than ever," was how German news service DPA summarized the latest annual report from Hamburg-based aviation safety information bureau JACDEC (Jet Airliner Crash Data Evaluation Center) in February 2009 .[147] In 2008, the world's 60 biggest airlines suffered two accidents; both were classified as minor. As a passenger nowadays, you have less to fear boarding a plane than you do getting in a cab at the airport taxi rank. And you can thank targeted measures aimed at controlling the "human factor" that have been put into place over the last three decades: Crew Resource Management.

MANY APPLICATIONS FOR CRM

In light of this successful track record, it should come as no surprise that other safety-critical industries have taken note of developments in aviation—

---

147 "Unfallstatistik: Große Fluglinien sind sicherer denn je" (Accident Statistics: Large Airlines Are Safer than Ever"), *Der Spiegel*, February 10, 2009, www.spiegel.de.

medicine, for example. Experts estimate that between 62 and 73 percent of all hospital "resuscitation incidents" are avoidable, according to Munich University Hospital's Institute for Emergency Medicine and Medicine Management, following analysis of an American study.[148] Their prescription is Team Resource Management. Put bluntly, two out of three resuscitation patients only have to be reanimated in the first place because someone screwed up. Relevant factors are noted as including "weekends, general wards, 'unsuitable' situations." Best have a heart attack on a weekday, then. American hospitals have introduced CRM programs that include nurses being taught to contradict operating surgeons.[149] The Austrian Armed Forces, the Bundesheer, has also looked at "increased security on deployment through Crew Resource Management." The US Department of Transportation has tested "Rail Crew Resource Management." At a German Society for Aeronautics and Astronautics (DGLR) conference, experts discussed the benefits of improved cooperation for sea travel, the railroads, in "high risk" organizations, and even during long-duration space missions.[150]

Company Resource Management

Wherever there is a risk to human life, it seems that people are prepared to hunt down potential sources of danger and to increase levels of cooperation. However, should it really be necessary for lives to be in danger before the most troublesome aspects of innate human responses and behavior are dealt with in a targeted and careful manner? These same response patterns and failures of perception and communication have just the same dangerous impact on perfectly "normal" businesses. There, they may not cost lives, but they often cost jobs and huge sums of money. Well-thought-out Company Resource Management may well

---

148 M. Ruppert et al., "Team Resource Management beim Krankenhausnotfall" (Team Resource Management at Hospital Emergencies), www.inm-online.de/pdf/aktuelles/veroeffentlichungen/divi2004_trm_kh-notfall.pdf.
149 "Crew Resource Management Benefits Doctors, Nurses, and Patients Alike," www.nurse-recruiter.com.
150 Michael Mikas, "Psychologie: Mehr Sicherheit im Einsatz durch Crew Resource Management" (Psychology: More Safety in Military Missions through Crew Resource Management), *Truppendienst*, no. 5 (2009), www.bundesheer.at; "Rail Crew Resource Management (CRM): Pilot Rail CRM Training Development and Implementation," www.fra.dot.gov/downloads/Research/ord0703-I.pdf; "Fachauschusssitzung Anthropotechnik:Kooperative Arbeitsprozesse," October 27–28, 2009.

prove as effective in warding off these dangers as CRM has at reducing the risk of air accidents.

The Concept

Ideas for this kind of Company Resource Management were developed in the last chapter. The key idea of "typical human factors" needs to be taken seriously and systematically integrated into the management process—rather than trying to simply ignore them by using purely technocratic or bureaucratic management techniques (or whatever the latest "management by . . ." trend might be). Those who refuse to factor them in to the management process will have to shoulder the costs down the line, and if they are unlucky, and the notorious "series of unfortunate events" is set in motion, then the repercussions could be heavy. Once caught up in this situation, sermons and mission statements are of little use. Tangible action is necessary. Let's consider the most important factors of Company Resource Management.

Minimize Stress Situations and Prepare in Advance: Avoid Stress

Stress multiplies mistakes—from perceptual errors to breakdowns in communication. The task of Company Resource Management here is to prevent extreme situations from developing, role-play crises (worst-case scenarios), identify critical factors (warning system), and develop contingency plans if/when the worst case does occur.

Avoiding Management Arrogance: Create a New Leadership Culture

Managers who are not held to account by any checks or balances risk coming unstuck thanks to their own arrogance. No one is immune to making mistakes, and at the management level, mistakes can have devastating consequences. Company Resource Management means establishing a leadership culture that listens to critical voices.

Set Targets, but Reevaluate Them Regularly: Be Realistic about Your Goals

As important as targets are, they can also blind you to risks. The more time and money invested in reaching a target, the greater the danger that the target becomes an obsession. Company Resource Management means avoiding fixation on arbitrary targets by using effective risk analysis, setting clear turning points, and being prepared to make an emergency landing—even when it seems like you are already within touching distance of the target.

Keep Your Eye on the Prize: Concentrate on What Is Most Important

Furious activity often conceals mental lethargy. Flurries of projects and pointless meetings might keep everyone busy, but they do nothing to keep the company in the black. Company Resource Management means keeping a constant eye on the numbers and external factors (situational awareness) and systematically identifying and eliminating redundant habits and processes ("spring cleaning"), as well as ensuring that decisions are put into practice in a controlled manner.

Clearly Define Roles: Delegate and Divide Tasks Sensibly

Who does what? If areas of responsibility are blurred and points of communication are lacking, chaos is inevitable. The bigger and more complex an organization, the more vital it is that tasks be assigned thoughtfully and professionally. Company Resource Management ensures that clear rules are in place for critical areas and that people truly take responsibility and take feedback into consideration (closed-loop principle).

Managing Mistakes: Aim for a "No-Blame" Culture

Although many companies like to boast of their "positive error culture," few of them have taken concrete steps to put it into practice. Company Resource Management means that errors are not punished; rather, concealing errors is punished. Clear routines exist for dealing with mistakes—and managers do not make exceptions for themselves.

Promote Good Communication: Communicate Openly and Fairly

If communication within a business breaks down, soon everything will break down. From killer phrases to threats, from withholding information and moaning to thoughtlessly agreeing with every suggestion, negative communication routines can infect a company, whether adopted consciously or simply without thinking.

Company Resource Management primes people for solution-oriented cooperation and puts a stop to killer phrases and the shutting down of contrary opinions.

In summary: Company Resource Management mobilizes all the resources a company needs to stay successful.

ABOUT THE AUTHOR

Professional pilot, businessman, communication expert, and management trainer: this is a CV that has helped make Peter Brandl one of the most in-demand public speakers based in Germany. He has spoken in 14 countries on three continents. Since 1993 he has been advising and training key individuals in the business community, covering areas such as communications, customer acquisition, negotiating techniques, and conflict management. His customers have been able to profit from his many years of experience in management as both sales director and managing director, during which time he started a second career as a professional pilot and flight instructor.

In his presentations and seminars, Peter Brandl combines management techniques with insights from the field of airline Crew Resource Management to produce one success-oriented whole. He reaches thousands of participants every year and is one of the Top 100 Excellent Speakers. His customers include blue chip names such as Audi, Commerzbank, Credit Suisse, IBM, Microsoft, Fresenius Medical Care, and MTU South Africa and also numerous upwardly mobile small and medium-sized enterprises (SMEs). Find out more at www.peterbrandl.com.

Printed in the USA
CPSIA information can be obtained
at www.ICGtesting.com
JSHW082229140824
68134JS00017B/807

9 781630 478049